An Orphan's Odyssey:

Half-Century through Revolution, War and Peace

A Memoir by

Kevork Manjikian

Translated and annotated by
Garabet K. Moumdjian
and
Marina Nercessian

Armenian edition edited by Hagop Hovsep Manjikian
Hamazkayin Armenian Educational and Cultural Society, 2008, Montreal, Canada
Dépôt légal: 4e trimestre, 2008. ISBN 2-921027-06-02

English edition edited by Hagop Hovsep Manjikian
All maps provided by Hagop Tcholakian
Family photos from Hagop Hovsep Manjikian's archive
ISBN-13: 979-8-9859807-0-7

Dedicated to the Republic of Armenia
and generations of Armenians and friends
who welcomed it in 1918.

Kevork (George) Manjikian
(1905-1985)

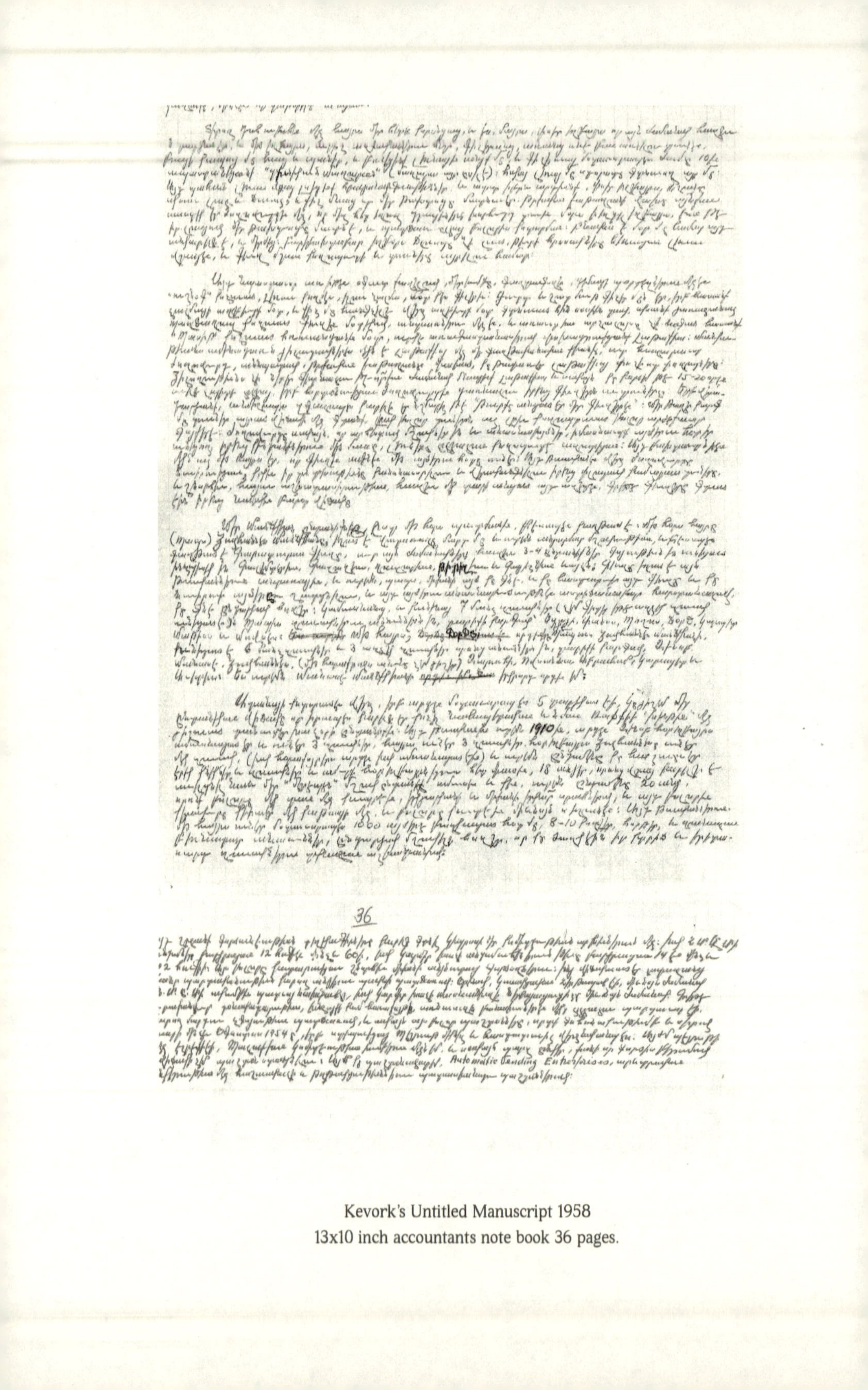

Kevork's Untitled Manuscript 1958
13x10 inch accountants note book 36 pages.

Table of Content

Introduction – International Edition

Armenian, Arabic, English, Turkish

Key Words: ***memory, working memory, episodic memory, identity, inter-generational memory, autobiography, historical-memory***

Human memory emerged as an unusual ***de novo force*** *on Earth when humans simultaneously, un-selfconsciously walked upright and spoke forthright. Fecundity of* ***working memory*** *is prodigious, ubiquitous. This force-function of human consciousness separates it from all other creatures on Earth. Working memory is individual, an inwardly imperial performative, that simultaneously structures childhood memory and individual identity by age five. As inter-generational memory takes hold already a linguistic umbilicus is functioning between parents, children and grandparents.*

Historical Timeflow

1874 Winston Churchill, Mehmed Talaat, birth
1882 Roupen der Minassian
1905 Kevork George Manjikian
1908 Young Turk Revolution
1909 Adana Massacres
1910 Winston Churchill meets Mehmed Talaat
1910 Mehmed Talaat meets Johannes Østrup
1914 Franz Ferdinand assassination June 28
1914 Mehmed Talaat meets Armen Garo June 30
1914 World War One (WWI) August 1
1914 Mehmed Talaat meets U.S. Ambassador Oct 29
1914 Turkey attacks Russia October 29
1914 Russia declares war on Turkey November 2
1917 Russian Revolution
1918 Republic of Armenia
1939 World War Two (WWII)
1946 Churchill, Cold War Declaration
1947 UN Partition of Palestine
1948 Arab-Jewish War
1956 Suez Canal England France Israel attack Egypt
1958 Kevork Memoir, Lebanon Political Crisis

Historical Memory: In Their Own Words

2008 Jivan R. Tabibian, Ambassador, Republic of Armenia: "*In politics the only identity that counts is who your parents are and who your children are, the rest is powder and rouge*"

1521 Nicolò Machiavelli, 'Art of War': "*If a sect or a republic is to survive for any length of time, it must return frequently to its beginning*"

1910 Winston Churchill's letter from Constantinople to Foreign Secretary **Edward Grey**: "*The only view I have formed about this part of the world of ruined civilizations and harshly jumbled races is this – **why can't England and Germany come together in strong action and for general advantage.***"

1910 Churchill between Talaat and Cavid (with fezzes) Constantinople Istanbul: Churchill Archives Centre, Broadwater Collection. Reproduced with permission of Curtis Brown, London.

1910 Mehmed Talaat meets Johannes Ostrup Danish diplomat: "*If I ever come to power in this country, I will use all my might to **exterminate the Armenians.***"

1914 Mehmed Talaat meets Armen Garo June 30: *Talaat asked, "Garo, why haven't you said anything tonight?" .... Garo:" You've taken the wrong road; your adopted course will lead the Ottoman Empire into an* *abyss. Intoxicated from your recent successes, you are carried away by a megalomania, imagining yourselves to be Napoleons and Bismarck's:"I am Bismarck", interrupted Talaat, smiling. .... Garo: "Was it not you who just a short while ago said that you will* ***Turkify the Kurds****?* ***How? By virtue of which of your cultural gifts****?*

1914 Mehmed Talaat declares to U.S. Ambassador Hans Morgenthau: "*German Ambassador Wangenheim, Enver and I all prefer that war should come now. (October 29)*".

1920 Avetik Isahakyan*: "Remove the veil from your eyes - the cruel truth will spread before your eyes - what Musavat could not do, Bolshevism realized.* ***Ittihad is a Bolshevik****, this is the reality. I have an undeniable fact that Talaat Pasha works among the Spartacus League workers in Berlin. You might not believe this, but it is just a real that* ***Mustafa Kemal inspires his masses with Bolshevism"***

Publisher's Words

Two ambitious imperial politicians, warlords Mehmed Talaat and Winston Churchill, shaped the trajectory of Kevork's life and times by their ardent pursuit of war when peace was a viable option.

World War I was Talaat's war, just as World War II was Churchill's war.

A third wartime leader Roupen der Minassian, a revolutionary warrior and former defense minister of Armenia also had a decisive influence on Kevork's life and times (Chapter 15).

My uncle and godfather, Kevork Manjikian, chronicled his extraordinary journey in two autobiographies.

The first, written at the age of 15, detailed his WWI odyssey during which he met a world in turmoil. He submitted this account in late December 1920 as part of his petition for admission to the Armenian Seminary of Jerusalem in Palestine.

His second memoir, written at the age of 53, reflected on his career as an expert in global naval trade and shipping. This time, he documented his encounters with the world in both peace and war, spanning interwar years in Palestine under British rule, WWII and the Middle East wars that followed under Cold War conditions.

In 1958, Lebanon faced a political crisis that threatened to ignite a civil war and escalate into a regional Middle East conflict. To prevent this, U.S. intervened by land and sea as USA Marines disembarked on Beirut beaches while astonished sun bathers looked on.

During this volatile crisis lasting three months Kevork felt compelled to document his life experiences as a tribute to his adopted father Roupen der Minassian (Chapter 15). Amid this political turmoil he penned a 35,000-word manuscript in a large 13×10-inch accountant's notebook—36 pages filled with history, insight and reflection.

My earliest memories of uncle Kevork date back to the 1948 War when I was four and a half years old.

At the time he lived in Haifa's Carmel Hills where he would drive me around in his car. Our family resided in Jaffa, one block from the Mediterranean Sea promenade.

On April 9th, 1948, after the Deir Yassin massacre, terror and fighting erupted uncontrollably between Arab and Jewish fighters and Jaffa came under bombardment. The British Army remained positioned between Jaffa and Tel Aviv.

During this chaos uncle Kevork took swift action. He packed two families—his sister Zabel's and brother Nishan's along with their children—into a military style canvas-covered truck.

Ten of us traveled with only mattresses and suitcases. Sitting beside the driver wearing short sleeve white shirt, Kevork led us to a military checkpoint, guiding us to safety. After the military check point he disappears in my memory but images remain.

There are two vivid photographic images printed in my mind, one is Kevork sitting beside the driver. I could see his back. He was wearing white short sleeve shirt, his right elbow resting on the window sill. The second image was at a military check point. I noticed across the road a soldier with his rifle lying face down on the ground beside a tank in a pool of blood (I must have been lifted out of the truck to be able to see across the road).

Unlike the rest of us who wanted to flee the violence, he decided not to flee. He refused to be intimidated at gunpoint, exiled, or ethnically cleansed as his family had been in 1909 and 1915 during WWI.

Instead, he returned to Haifa, where he became an Israeli citizen living there until 1954, when he was coerced into leaving to Beirut, becoming a Palestinian-Israeli refugee.

We had not seen Uncle Kevork since the 1948 War. But in the summer of 1954 my father and I greeted him at the Lebanon-Israel border. He was "forced" to leave Israel under circumstances that, in hindsight, were politically driven.

Kevork explained that Israeli authorities were pleased to see him leave for two reasons. He had successfully evaded Israel's strict censorship of outgoing mail, ensuring that news about the Armenian community in Israel did not reach the outside world. He also had fought—albeit unsuccessfully—to reclaim his property in West Jerusalem, which settlers had confiscated. The Municipality of Jerusalem had even issued him a construction permit for a three-story residential building on Allenby Street in the Katamon district, West Jerusalem, but he was never able to reclaim his land parcel.

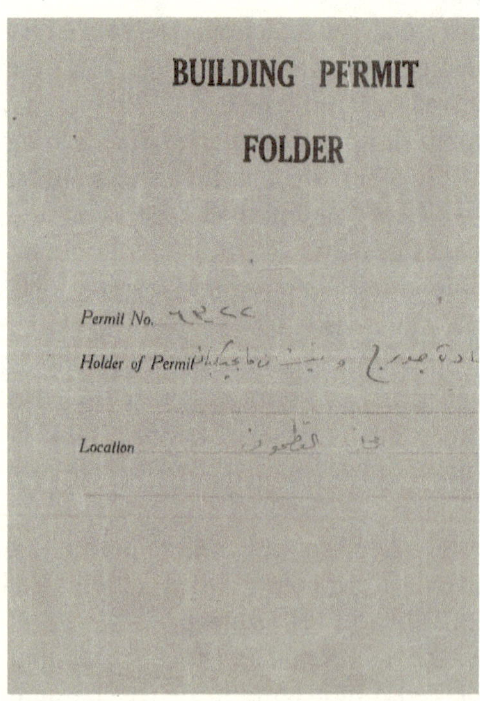

BUILDING PERMIT

FOLDER

Permit No.

Holder of Permit

Location

Ammo Kevork was a man of action, acutely aware of the prevailing authorities around him. In 1948 May-June anarchy period, once Israeli State was in charge, Kevork even approached Israeli State leader David Ben-Gurion. However he was only able to get through to Ben-Gurion's Secretary.

Millions of ordinary people experienced the historical period that Kevork documents as his own life and times.

We are pleased to share his "time capsule" autobiography with all those who are descendants of individuals who also had lived during Kevork's life and times.

******

Eric Margolis, *quoting* ***Benjamin Franklin****: 'No Bad Peace; No Good Wars'* "I consider World War I the greatest tragedy to befall civilization. World War II may have killed more civilians, but World War I killed or wounded more soldiers and destroyed much of Europe after a century of glittering civilization"

Zaven Manjikian
2025, Yerevan, Armenia

PUBLISHER'S CITIZENSHIP

1943-1948	1948-1956	1956-present	2014-Present
Palestine	Refugee - Lebanon	U.S.A.	Armenia

GOVERNMENT OF PALESTINE.
DEPARTMENT OF HEALTH
Certificate of Registration of Birth
No. 316702

Birth certificate, Palestine 1943

BIBILIOGRAPHY

Baer, Marc David (2010). '*The Dönme, Jewish Converts, Muslim Revolutionaries, and Secular Turks*'. Stanford University Press.

Baer, Marc David (2020). '*Sultanic Saviors and Tolerant Turks, Writing*

ACKNOWLEDGEMENT ARMENIAN EDITION

The publishing of this book is a spiritual compensation to a kind and caring couple, Kevork and Yeghisapet Manjikian, who played the role of second parents during my years of education. There is also the important aspect of this volume representing the struggles and achievements of a Genocide survivor and Palestine Armenian Diaspora's ever-changing life.

Kevork Manjikian's memoir is written in one breath, clear in a beautiful handwriting, and in a chronological sequence. The division of the chapters, the retouching of the language, and adaptations have been made so that the reading of the original text would be fluent, always attempting to keep the general style and characteristics of the text.

For the publication of this volume, I thank the Hamazkayin Educational and Cultural Association's Canadian Regional Executive which accepted to include this book in its publication series. A special thank-you to Hagop Garabed Manjikian, Kevork's cousin, who wrote the introduction and made valuable addendums and comments; to Haroutiun Berberian for his suggestions to improve the first draft; to Levon Der Minassian, Roupen's son who read the chapter "With Roupen Der Minassian" and encouraged that this volume be published; and to Vrej-Armen Artinian who edited the final draft.

Hagop Hovsep Manjikian
2008, Montreal, Canada

PREFACE ARMENIAN EDITION

Kevork Manjikian's manuscript of recollections is a welcome addition to the collections of Armenian memorabilia literature. Independent of the circumstances of the author's or his immediate family's histories, it has more than one universal value, especially those segments related to the Armenian Genocide; when placed side by side, they constitute crucial evidence for our history.

Kevork begins his memoirs with his childhood years by reproducing his impressions of the natural environment in his birthplace village, the events and episodes he had witnessed.

The first three chapters of the volume are dedicated to the description of his family and the general village life: patriarchal customs, habits, and occupation. Here he covers the Manjikian family origin and the events that occurred in the birthplace village of Karadouran (or Kaladouran).

The important segment of the memoirs is the sections on the 1915 deportation from his village. This constitutes one of the links of the chain of the Armenian Genocide history. Kevork introduces the events in the fourth and fifth chapters by recounting how, on July 30 of 1915, under the orders of the Turkish government, 20 members of his Grandfather Gergeoss' (George, Kevork) family and 1,400 compatriots from nearby Armenian villages are all banished from their peaceful abodes and under the watch of the police are deported towards Southern Syria and Transjordan.

In the scorching heat of summer, after walking for 600 kilometers through unknown territory in unbearable heat and losing all of their belongings, the deported arrive in Amman, Transjordan, and then disperse to nearby villages. The exhaustion, hardship, hunger, spiritual torment, and strains physically consume the deported, destroying their will and stamina. This tortuous condition changes to a disaster when the immigrants are infected with typhus. Within a few weeks, the 9 out of 20 members of Kevork's grandfather's family fall victims to this epidemic. The family is turned into a pitiful wreck of helpless widows and orphans, while only three months earlier in the calm valley of Mount Cassius on the shore of the Mediterranean Sea, the family had been living peacefully.

In his memoirs, Kevork doesn't include any hideous scenes depicting the carnage of the bloody massacres or the live burnings nor any depictions of horror or terror. Nevertheless, the book is a true testimony of subjecting a huge mass of people to deportation to starvation to epidemics by the insidious means carried out by the Turkish government. The rest of the book is Kevork's life story from the day he was orphaned until he wrote his memoir in 1958.

There are two notable segments which we would like to refer to separately. Chapter 8, "My Mother Recounts," is a heartbreaking account of the genocide. This is the lamentation of an unfortunate woman who is expatriated by force to a faraway world; she loses her husband and newborn to a typhus epidemic and her baby to malnutrition and starvation, is tormented by the reality of raising her five minor infants on her own, hopeless, alone, and in the mercy of fate. An irrefutable testimony to the genocidal deeds that the Turkish government perpetrated in 1915, in Asia Minor and the deserts of Arabia.

Chapter 15, "With Roupen Der Minassian," presents a different nuance of the book. Hosting the famous revolutionary and his wife in his home for three and a half years, Kevork Manjikian writes, "These were the happiest years of my life," having reached a dignified life after a poor and wretched beginning. Indeed, this segment that covers one tenth of the volume gives an added value to the memoir. For anyone who is acquainted with Roupen's revolutionary and literary works, new revelations can be found here, which shed further light to the character of the Armenian revolutionary and his works.

On this occasion, we find it appropriate to register the following: one of the Armenian schools in Akhalkalaki (Javakhk, Georgia) during the Soviet Union, and through 1998, was known as School Number 5. Having had no state funding for approximately 10 years, the school facilities suffered serious damage. A sum was allocated from the will of Kevork and Yeghisapet Manjikian for renovating and improving the school building. In appreciation for the respect that Kevork and Yeghisapet had toward the great native of Akhalkalaki (Roupen was born in Akhalkalaki), the school administration renamed the school the Roupen Der Minassian Armenian School.

Kevork wrote his memoir in 1958, in Beirut, Lebanon. He lived for 27 more years until 1985, and never wrote anything further. His nephew, Hagop Hovsep Manjikian, publisher of this volume, completed that void in the epilogue.

Kevork Manjikian was a man with a good heart, a kind and magnanimous personality, a warm character, and had a clean lifestyle. He had a happy childhood, an unfortunate adolescence, a robust, tough, and active youth. In his adult life, he lived loving his relatives and kinfolks; helping the needy and those unable to help themselves, serving national and noble purposes.

His memoir now belongs to the Armenian nation.

Hagop Garabet Manjikian
December 2007
Los Angeles, California, USA

4 km

Panoramic view of the Karadourann Valley on the southern slope of mount Casius.
Left to right: Seashore is the Syrian-Turkish border. To its North Mousa Dagh at a distance and Mount Casius. To its East is the Kessab Township.

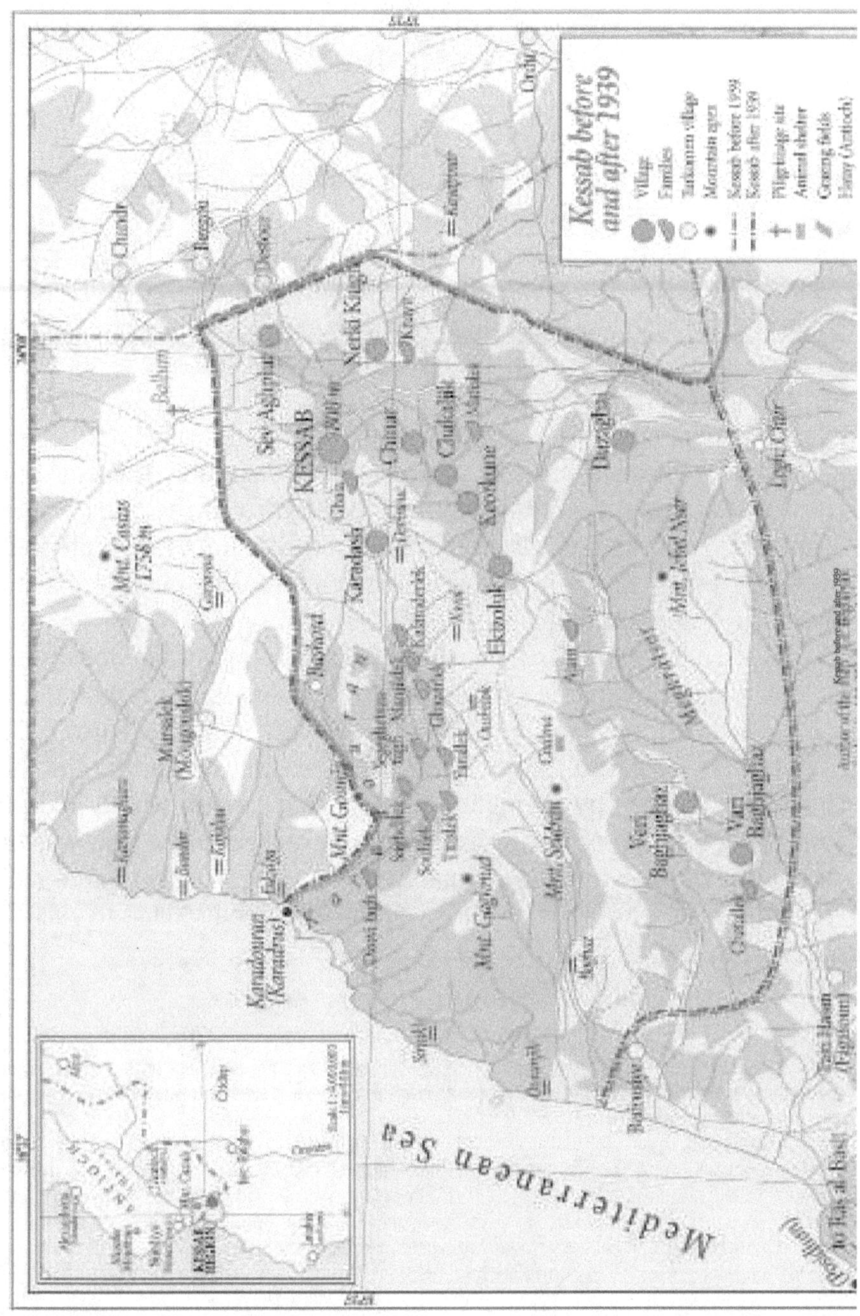
Kessab before and after 1939
KESSAB
Mediterranean Sea

Chapter 1

THE BEGINNING YEARS

I was born on August 25, 1905, in Karadouran, a village in Kessab region on the slopes of Mount Casius.[1]

The first shocking event of my childhood was the 1909 Adana massacres,[2] when all the villages in the Kessab region were attacked by neighboring Turkish villagers, and Armenians were forced to flee and take refuge in the impregnable mountains of Kessab, from where they moved to the nearest city, Latakia.[3]

In this turmoil my father lost track of our family. My mother, my (two-year-old) younger brother, my older brother, and I, along with other relatives at night, without taking anything from the house except for loaves of bread and some cheese, took the road to a mountain pass. Late at night we sheltered in a cave called Dunigun Maghiran, located at the base of a huge mountain.

At that moment we heard gunshots from the mountain tops. As a result, my younger brother, Nishan, started crying and screaming, and we came close to revealing our hideout. The terror of the Turkish fire and sword was so feared that the neighbors beside us asked my mother to silence my brother by strangling him, so that no one would find our hideout and be the cause of our group massacre. Naturally, that was not possible for a mother to do. Fortunately for us, the Turkish bandits did not hear my brother's screams and went down to the village to rob and pillage homes.

1 Kessab region is an Armenian only off shore enclave centered by mount Casius with a township and surrounding villages. Karadouran valley extends from seashore 9 kilometers inland to the township. (see photos and maps, pages 18-19).

2 In 1909, catastrophic massacres took place within the Armenian-populated provinces, such as Adana, Aleppo, and others found throughout the Ottoman Empire. The Massacre of Adana was the most unspeakable since more than 20 thousand killed. The calamity of Kessab began on Friday April 23 till 26 in 1909. A mob from Ordou attacked Kessab township and surrounding villages. Turkoman mob attacked the township and its villages, township residents resisted the attack for eight hours to allow the people to seek safer grounds and eventually find their way west to the seashore. (Tcholakian, H. [1995]. Kessab, Vol. 1 [pp. 89-98]. Syrian Regional Administration of Hamazkayin.)

3 Latakia is a port city 55 km south of Kessab (see map, page 19).

1909 Adana massacre, kessab township population escape route through Karadouran valley to the sea shore.

Predawn view from Chalma plateau to Basit peninsula.

Around midnight, and taking advantage of this opportunity, our group made its way stealthily through the orchards facing us and along the slope of Oushnok plateau, which ascends toward the mountaintop plain of Chalma.[1] It was a cold and very dark night when we arrived at the Chalma spring. After resting under the old sycamore tree near the spring for a while, we continued our descent toward the village of Baghjaghaz. From there we came to the Basit[2] peninsula harbor, and then we sailed by schooner to the Latakia harbor.

One of the bitter memories of my childhood is our lives as deportees in Latakia, where thousands of people fleeing the Turkish bloodshed aimlessly wandered in the dusty streets. I do not recall how long we stayed in Latakia, but I think it wasn't more than 15-20 days, when the people were allowed to return[3] to their houses and villages.

1 Chalma plateau on the slope of Mount Seldran, is famous for its ice-cold spring and majestic sycamore tree. To this day, this spring and tree remains a touristic landmark.

2 On the morning of April 24, refugees from Karadourann and other villages assembled on Basit peninsula beach. Some in small fishing boats sail to Latakia harbor 55 miles south. The British and French consulates in Latakia and the director of the American Hospital in there, James Balf, organized the evacuation of 7000 refugees who sheltered in the American Girls' School, in the fortress, in the Latin Church, and in the Armenian Rest Home. (Tcholakian [1995], pp. 89-98).

3 On May 2-3 1909, the people of Kessab returned to Basit on 3 battleships: the Italian Piedmont, the French Michelet, and the Jule Ferry. Those whose homes were burned sheltered in tents. There were 160 deaths. The Turks torched 1,544 houses and looted 5,604 houses. (ibid)

Chalma Plateau

A 1909 photograph taken in Karaduran, Manjikians district, on the patio of the mayor's two-story home, which was burned during the Adana Massacres.

When we returned to our village, it became clear that the Turks had passed through. Some of the homes in our neighborhood were burnt down, and the rest were completely looted of their valuables. But the people, who were farmers or herders, immediately set about rebuilding their lives. The majority of goats were saved because they were in the mountain grazing fields. One of those lucky herd owners was my Grandfather George, who had the largest herd of goats in the village. The villagers committed themselves to resurrect their farming economy and rebuilding their ruined or burnt houses. And thanks to the traditional diligence of the Armenians, barely a year after the catastrophe, the villages had mostly recovered.

As told to me by my Grandfather George, our Manjikian ancestors lived in Kessab Township. His father, my Great-grandfather Hovhannes Manjikian,[4] whom we called *Bebo* or *Babook,* was a sickly man and thus unable to work the land. He decided to move to Karadouran, where four to five families lived, such as the Kalemderians, the Kazazians, the Ghazarians, the Titizians, and the Kairchians. At that time the Karadouran village was forested. So, my great-grandfather bought a few goats and settled in the village and dedicated his time to rearing the goats. Gradually he got rich through goat herding and was able to buy large tracts of arable land (for growing livestock, which increased the family's wealth and standing).

My Great-grandfather Hovhannes married and had seven sons, like his father, Yessayi I[5], along with three daughters. His seven sons were, in order of birth, Yessayi , Boghos, Garabet, George, Matios, Panos, and Moussa. My Grandfather George had only six sons and three daughters, whose names, in birth order were Zenop, Minas, Hovhannes, Zerdi, Zarouhi, Mari, Apraham, Garabet, and Avedis. I am Minas Manjikian's second son.

After the Adana massacre, when I was about five years old, I remember how the condition of my family was a traditional patriarchy, three generations living under one roof, similar to the household in Danouder Khacho's family, a character in the novel *Khente* (*The Fool*) by the Armenian novelist Raffi.[6] By 1910, my senior uncle, Zenop, was already

4 The Manjikian surname originates from a man nicknamed "Manjik," a 19th-century trader who dealt in Kessab's cash crops, such as tobacco and laurel oil. He transported these goods by schooner from the Karaduran seashore to Alexandria, Egypt, where he sold them following Napoleon's conquest. According to folklore, his nickname derives from the Italian verb mangiare or the French manger, both meaning "to eat." Over generations, this nickname evolved into the surname Manjikian. See Appendix, (Tcholakian, H. [2015]. Kessab, Western Armenia, Cilicia, Number 8 [pp. 120–122].)

5 Yessayi I, his son Hovhannes, and his grandson Yessayi II each had seven male offspring. See Appendix.

6 Armenian writer, Hakob Meliq-Hakobian (aka Raffi, 1835-1888) wrote about the Armenians' struggle to liberate themselves from their oppressors. In one of his books, he describes a traditional family: " ...the

married and had three children. My father, Minas, already had three children, my Uncle Hovhannes had one child, and my three aunts were already married. The number of family members reached 18: husbands, wives, children, and single uncles. In addition to them, we also had a *maraba* (farmhand[7]) and his wife, who helped out with farm work. So, all in all, 20 people lived in the same two-story house. Our meals were prepared in one big pot, and all of us sat at the same table to eat.

In those years, my Grandfather Gergeoss (George, Kevork) had a large herd of goats in the hundreds, 8-10 cows, calves, and various animals of burden, and extensive tracks of farmland, which flourished with the hard work of his brave and young children.

It was pleasant to see my father and my three uncles, the ploughs on their shoulders, heading to the fields early in the morning, following the oxen. But my grandfather would spend almost all year in the mountains with the shepherds, with a hunting rifle on his shoulder. It was also nice to see the housewives: one would milk the cows, the other would bake bread or do chores (child rearing, house cleaning, help in harvesting in the fields or gardens), and the third would carry water from a nearby spring, a pair of water jugs on her shoulders, lowering her headscarf, a see-through veil, to her nose. My two younger uncles, Garabet and Avedis, headed to school down the street along with my cousin, Serop, and my brother, Hovsep.

This is all I remember of my family's life from my childhood. Now it seems to me that that was the authentic patriarchal way of living. Full of admiration, I would see my brother go to school, holding a book bag full of different snacks and dried fruits. The other little ones and I made mischief in the front yard. Days would go by happily. When I was five, I started school with a new book bag and primer. The pictures, sketches, and alphabet in the primer made a great impression on me.

I would like to share with you some of my childhood adventures. As I said, my grandfather spent all his time in the mountains with the shepherds and the goats. But he would come home during the Christian

outstanding possessions of old Khacho were his seven sons.... Six were married and the house overflowed with their children and their children's children. So old Khacho had several generations growing up around him, all living together, working together...." (Raffi [2000]. The Fool [Khente]. [Kimberly McFarlane & Beyon Miloyan, Translators.] Sophene Pty Ltd. [Original work published 1880])

7 A land tiller is a laborer who worked in lieu of one fourth of the harvest. Armenian marabas from Kessab also worked on fields belonging to Turkish and Greek landowners in nearby villages.

holy days, especially on Christmas and Easter. We waited impatiently for our grandfather, who was a very kind person. We were aware that he would bring the grandchildren many surprises from the mountains and his hunting. We anticipated his return, and when we saw him from afar, we would run to him. He would greet us by lifting and hugging, kissing, and petting each one of us. He would rest on a boulder and line us up, facing him like schoolchildren. Then would begin his questions to us. "Now, tell me, son, what would you want me to give you from my bag?"

Chalma - Spring - Sycamore Tree, circa 2006

So would begin our excitement: one would want a rabbit, the other would want a partridge. Recalling our preferences, he would pull out from that fascinating and unforgettable bag of his, partridges, rabbits, and birds that he had hunted and sometimes those that were alive. Surrounding him, we would bring home the good news of our grandfather's return full of gifts.

In the absence of our grandfather, my mother and my aunts, who took care of us, scolded us or forbade us to do this or that or not to run around, but their attitude would change the second our grandfather returned home. They would quietly approach the senior authority of the household and one by one kiss his hand, lifting their see-through veil face covering. As soon as our grandfather would sit down, surrounded by his grandchildren, one of my aunts would approach and silently remove his boots from his feet. Another aunt would come with a towel, pouring hot water in a tub so my grandfather could wash his feet.

After this ritual was completed and when his sons returned from the fields, in order of seniority they would approach grandfather, kiss his hand, and ask about his well-being. Later when everyone washed the dust from the field off themselves, the legendary tablecloth was spread on the floor, laden with what nature, with God's blessing, had provided. It was the duty of the first-born son to recite a prayer before eating dinner, and each mother would sit beside her children and begin eating. The women never spoke during dinnertime. His sons spoke only when Grandfather asked questions.

We, the children, were accustomed to these rules. After completing our silent dinner and a little play in the yard, we would go to bed. After quarrelling with one another, my brother and I were deep in sleep, happy with the gifts our grandfather had brought us that day. After enjoying the holidays at home, my grandfather would return to the mountain grazing fields, noting various gift requests of his grandchildren, happy and satisfied.

It must be said that my grandmother (née Ghazarian) was a physically and mentally strong woman and the actual manager of the house. Despite the fact that the daughters-in-law, by tradition, would not initiate a conversation with my grandmother, after a while she would insist that they speak to her directly and not to use sign language, which was the patriarchal custom of that time. On many occasions, my grandmother would accompany her husband to the mountains to help him, particularly when the goats were birthing. She would supervise the milking of goats and production of cheese, butter, and cream. Many times I went with my grandmother to *uba* (a huge tent made of goat hair carpets), where giant gallons of milk, yogurt, cream, and butter were stored along with goat hair, topsy-turvy. The premium butter with *lavash* (home baked bread) was set aside for the grandchildren.

These mountain visits were the most precious moments of freedom in our lives, when we would roam freely in the mountains, in the uba, or in the fields nearby, where we would find perfect freedom, free of my mother's scorns. With the encouragement and approval of my grandmother, we would sometimes visit the billy goats' pen to see the newborn kids, play with them, and even claim ownership of several. Naturally our uba visits took place during school and religious holidays.

When I was eight, we had a neighborhood gang to fight boys from another neighborhood, sometimes by throwing rocks at them or beating them up and sometimes being beaten up by them.

My father, Minas, in spite of graduating elementary school and continuing his education by learning Arabic for one year in Latakia, chose to join his farmer brothers. My father was very strict with me and had to be much more so because of my mischief-making. As a result, I was very often thrashed.

My mischief went up a notch during the fruit-ripening season in the orchards. I have to say I was one of the better students in my school, but when the trees began to bear fruit, some of my classmates and I would hide our school bags in bushes and spend the entire day walking in the orchards, sampling semi-ripened fruits. And in the evenings, one of our classmates would let us know what the assignments were for the following day. We would then study hard, and when my father would ask me to read the assignment, he would realize that I had completed my homework.

One time I recall how for almost a week we were absent from school and when the teacher, assuming that I was ill, spotted my father and asked him if I were ill. My father told him that I was at school because he would ask me to read a lesson and that I knew my assignment. It was then that my teacher explained to my father that "Kevork was never present at the school for an entire week." That evening, my father casually asked me where I had been that morning. I confidently answered that I had been at school. Having my lies exposed, I was punished and reprimanded for my repeated lies. I was unable to indulge in the pleasure of eating more of the fruits for the rest of that season.

Chapter 2
PATRIARCHAL HEARTH

One day when I was nine years old, my grandfather returned home as usual during a holiday. After the family dinner, he called all his sons upstairs to the *oda* (living room, Turkish), informing them he had a serious issue to discuss. All six sons, who had never seen their father this serious, looked at each other in astonishment and obediently followed him upstairs.

As both a favorite of my grandfather and curious about this gathering, I followed my grandfather upstairs and was permitted to sit next to him. So solemn was my grandfather that without any introduction, he said to his sons, "Realizing that the family members have increased in number, and this house has become inadequate for us all, I have decided to separate you from each other and share my possessions with all of you. In order to avoid any future misunderstandings, I will divide my possessions in your presence, in equal parts, and with your approval. So, my son, Minas, since you are the most schooled, take a piece of paper, divide it into seven equal parts, and write on each one what I have to say."

My father Minas wrote on each of the seven pieces of paper, identifying names of the planting fields (tobacco, wheat), orchards, vegetable gardens, tillable parcels of land, and particular trees in those fields. Having received the approval of all six sons regarding the fairness of this method of dividing the possessions he concluded, "My sons, you see that I have tried to divide equally all my possessions, and each one will get what is listed on each piece of paper by drawing lots. In the future, I do not want you to have disputes, claiming your portions were good or bad. I do this so that you avoid any family feud. Since I have not drawn lots yet, I would like you to tell me if you want to make any further changes (to the method of drawing lots or contents of the divisions), so that it will be approved by all of you."

My father and his brothers made a number of recommendations and changes, and after their consent my grandfather removed his *fes* (hat) and placed those seven pieces of paper in it; that is, six pieces of papers for the sons and one piece of paper for him and my grandmother. Then turning to me, he said, "My beloved, pick a piece of paper and give it to your Uncle Zenop," and so each son received his land inheritance as written down on the paper.

After this ritual my grandfather, as the senior authority of the family, blessed the sons and declared that each one must be satisfied with his share, good or bad, and each had to try to develop and improve his possessions with his own effort. He admonished his sons not to disagree among themselves over the land holdings, thus maintaining the family status and honor.

As for the livestock — goats, cows, oxen, donkeys, horses — my grandfather declared, "As long as I am alive, they will be under my care on the condition that each of you will receive from me all your annual dairy needs, such as fat, butter, yogurt, cheese, milk, as much as needed. And now I assign that the two older brothers, Zenop and Minas, take on the responsibility of building the four new homes as soon as possible, sharing the construction costs: each for my three married sons, Zenop, Minas, and Hovhannes, and another one for my fourth son, Apraham, whom I intend to marry off soon. And my two younger children, Garabet and Avedis, who are still minors, will stay in their parents' house, together with the farmhand."

So in the simplest and most patriarchal way, without any rancour or complaints, my grandfather distributed his possessions. According to his wishes, my father and senior uncle, Zenop, immediately began building four new houses, and my other two younger uncles, Hovhannes and Apraham, did the farming that year until the houses were built. After moving each household's belongings to new homes, my grandfather with a blessing and a kiss sent his sons to their newly built homes with their wives and children. To this day, as I write these lines — in 1958 — it seems that my grandfather's legitimate authority is firmly anchored in our hearts. There has never been a dispute over property in our family.

A new life began for us, the little ones, in our new one-story and two-room house, which was originally built at the edge of the village on the main road next to a stable for our cow and donkey. In the beginning everything seemed to be strange for us, as if being foreigners in that new house. We always missed our grandfather's house and the extended family. We felt lonely in our new house, which seemed unsuitable for our games. Until we got used to our new environment, we would escape and play in Grandfather's front yard.

Kessab Township, looking north toward Mount Casius, 2005

Karadouran, 2005

My father was a very kind and God-fearing man, even though he was strict with us. Every Sunday before breakfast he would take my older brother and me to church. He would insist that we wear, like him, the deacon's robes and serve on the altar. After the mass, along with my father, we would return home and have breakfast. Often our breakfast would be our lunch, which would include cracked wheat with chickpeas and lots of liquid yogurt called *tahn*.

In 1912, Uncle Apraham was going to get married. The family was in a festive mood. Several huge pots (cauldrons) lined my grandfather's yard, where the *harissa* wedding meal (a traditional Armenian dish with whole wheat kernels and shredded meat boiled to a porridge-like consistency) was being cooked. Several male goats were ritually slaughtered. The aroma of barbecue had taken over the village. The youth were eating and drinking — young men and women dancing the traditional Kessab circle dance on the rooftop of the house around a bonfire. The dancers were accompanied by melodies played by traditional folkloric instruments, *ghaval* and *davul-zurna*. They danced rhythmically, sometimes swaying, other times amiably moving shoulder to shoulder and pounding on the rooftop with their steps. Everyone participated on this wedding-eve circle dance.

On that autumn Sunday morning all the people in the village as well as relatives and acquaintances of nearby villages had gathered around a huge tablecloth. After eating the traditional wedding meal of harissa with *ghiima* (cooked minced meat), the youngsters headed to the village of Baghjaghaz in a dancing and singing procession.[1] They were going to bring the bride from her village.

We, the little ones, did not have permission to go that far. How could we stay at home? Therefore, in the afternoon with my playmates we, without anyone knowing, headed to Chalma Trail to greet the bridal party. After two o'clock in the afternoon the wedding party was visible descending from the direction of Chalma.

1 The village tradition calls for the bridal party to have an early lunch with some drinks, followed by a signing ceremony to dress the bridegroom usually the jacket and tie then the singing and dancing procession departs to bride's village. At bride's home the dancing and singing continues at higher pitch while the bride herself is being dressed including hairdo, crown, and veil, followed by mounting the bride on a horse and the procession returns to the bridegroom's church.

1912 uncle Apraham mountain trail wedding procession.
From Karadouran to Chalma Plateau to Baghjahaz bride's village; five hour round trip walk.

Baghjaghaz, circa 2005

The bride was sitting on a white horse, her face completely covered with a sheer fabric of see-through lace. My father was leading the bride, holding the horse reins in hand. My father had a smile on his face, signaling that we could join the wedding party. You could not imagine our excitement that we had finally gained enough maturity to join the wedding procession. Some of the young men danced on the roadside, and others who were partially drunk were wobbling while walking. And so with such festivity as we approached the village, it seemed the entire village joined the procession marching toward the church.

Near the church door Father Bedros Paboujian[2] greeted the bridal party at the church door. My father gingerly lifted the bride off the horse and led her to the waiting groom. The hymnody starts, and before the formal wedding ceremony, I noticed my father and the priest whispering to each other. Then their voices got louder, and I heard my father's angry words, "If she doesn't accept, then let her remove the gown and return to her father's house."

The murmuring increased. It surfaced that because the bride was from a Protestant family, my father and the priest insisted that she first must be baptized according to Armenian Apostolic Church tradition and then wed. But the bride and her family refused. That is why my father, who was going to be the best man as well, wanted to cancel the wedding. After a few moments of give and take, the bride finally accepted to be baptized, after which the church marriage ceremony was completed.

After the church ceremony, they lifted the bride on the white horse and resumed their singing and dancing procession, and the people celebrated their way to the couple's new built home. According to custom the bride did not immediately enter the house because of other rites that needed to be completed. A pomegranate was given to the bride, who had to throw it against the wall. If the fruit was smashed into many pieces, it was a sign that the bride was healthy and strong and could do her duties.

Then the best man, with a jug filled with sweets, crashed it on the threshold of the house, and the children jumped on those sweets to collect them. And still the bride would not enter the house, because now was the father-in-law's turn to deliver his gift. Until he delivered that gift

2 Father Bedros born in 1861 he was abbot of Kaladouran village residing in the Manjikian quarter. With most of his parish he repatriated to Soviet Armenia in 1947 and passed away in1948. (Tcholakian [2015], p. 485).

the bride could not enter the house. The shouting would begin, "Where is the father-in-law?"

My grandfather was elated and happy. He approached the bride and announced his personal gifts, such as this or that orchard or tillable land. Everyone applauded. After that, when the bride was about to set foot on the threshold, a lamb was ritually sacrificed, and only then the bride entered the groom's house. The guests then individually congratulated the newlyweds and joyfully departed.

From my childhood this village wedding was the most firmly anchored in my mind. Growing up I witnessed countless weddings with old and new customs; however, not one of them impressed me so much as my Uncle Apraham's wedding, which was authentic and loyal to its ancient rural village and patriarchal customs.

Chapter 3

THE RED HORSE

My uncles, especially Zenop and Hovhannes, loved to keep horses. At that time, we had a very likeable horse, reddish brown with a patch of diamond-shape white hair on its forehead. We all cherished this horse, especially my youngest uncle, Avedis, who often rode it to school with the farmhand.

It was said that this noble animal was the finest horse in the entire Kessab region and, therefore, everyone's favorite. It was such a loyal and compliant animal that when we, the little ones, jumped from a wall to its bare back, the kind animal would give in to our whims and trot gently without pulling us down from its back, as if he were our friend. However, when one of my uncles would ride it, realizing that the rider was a young adult, it would prance as if it wanted to gallop in an attempt to throw my uncle off of its back. Its only other young loved ones were my uncles, Zenop and Hovhannes, as well as my youngest uncle, Avedis, to whom the animal was especially connected.

When they did not need the horse, they would take it to the nearby hills and let it graze alone. And in the evening, at about the same time as the sun set, it would return home by itself and would start snorting to let us know that it was back.

One day in 1913, when the horse was left alone in the mountains to graze, it didn't return home at the usual time. My uncles went everywhere to look for it, but there was no sight of it anywhere. From another village someone reported that he had sighted Al Hawa, who was one of the well-known bandits in the area, so my uncles started to suspect that Al Hawa might have stolen it. Searching far and near, they confirmed that Al Hawa had indeed stolen the horse and had sold it to a Turkish Bey (chief government official) in Aleppo.

Despite the pleas of my father and grandfather, Uncle Avedis left for Aleppo. He found the horse and presented himself to the Turkish Bey, asking him to either return the horse that was stolen from them or if he could consider buying back his own horse. But the Turk Bey shouted the word *gyavur*[1] at my uncle and hit him. My uncle returned home despondent and explained what happened in Aleppo to his brother Zenop. Very upset with this feeling of hopelessness, they decided to take revenge on Al Hawa and, in due time, this incident was forgotten.

One spring night in 1914, when my father had traveled to Mersin,[2] and we were all asleep, Uncle Garabet, who was my mother's favorite, came to our house at 10 at night and started speaking to my mother in a hushed tone. As luck would have it, I hadn't fallen asleep but pretended to be. I perked my ears, trying to hear their whispers.

Mersin, before WWI

"You know, my dear one, my brother Zenop and *Ammo* (Uncle) Stepan Kalemderian have apprehended Al Hawa and imprisoned him in Uncle Zenop's stable. They plan to kill him."

My mother was disturbed with this account and pleaded, "Oh, my son, don't you dare say this to anyone else. Our family will be doomed."

They continued speaking in even lower tones. I was overwhelmed with fear. How would they kill Al Hawa (that well-known thief of our

1 *Infidel* a Turkish word denoteing non-muslems as unbelievers, to denigrate them as officially inferiors.
2 Pre WWI Mersin, Adana province. (see map page 45).

childhood imagination), especially when he was right next door in Uncle Zenop's stable, never mind that he was tied down and restrained? My childhood imagination could not grasp the full implications of the goings-on. However, since Uncles Zenop and Stepan had a reputation as strongest and bravest in our village, they were about to become my real heroes.

Zenop Manjikian, 1943
Kevork's eldest uncle before repatriating to Soviet Armenia in1947

The next morning, my mother sent my brother Hovsep and me to the garden to collect mulberry leaves to feed for the silkworms.[3] Last night's secret talk was very interesting, and I was still terrified. I was seeing Al Hawa everywhere and unable to resist the urge to share this secret with my brother Hovsep, even though we had fought the night before, which was the reason I was still awake and heard that ghastly news.

"Hovsep, do you know that Uncles Zenop and Stepan had caught Al Hawa and have killed him...?"

My brother said, "Shhh, don't you dare repeat that again. I, too, heard

3 Mulberry orchards were cultivated until the 1940s. Silk less worms were used as fishing bate.

it. I was also awake. Didn't you hear what your mother said to your uncle? Our family will be doomed if this news gets out."

Stepan Kalemderian with his granddaughters: Maro and Sona.
Karadouran, circa 1946

Months later, Uncle Zenop was arrested with a few other innocent people. Since there wasn't enough evidence, they were set free. Since then and for many years to follow, I had never uttered a word about that incident. However, at the end of World War I, when Turkey had been defeated and April 24, the Armenian Genocide had taken place, and we were exiles in Port Said tent city, I asked Uncle Zenop to tell me about that night's happenings in detail, and this was what he related:

"After our noble horse was stolen, I swore to myself that wherever I saw Al Hawa, I would catch him and make him confess that he had indeed stolen our beloved horse as I had presumed. Then I would, in fact, kill him. One evening when I was returning home from the fields, the plough on my shoulders following the oxen at dusk, I noticed someone in the distance. He was moving in our direction, sometimes hiding under the terrace walls. Further downhill I saw my friend Ammo-Stepan Kalemderian and told him 'I think Al Hawa is here. Would you join me so we can catch him?'

"So we put down our ploughs at the edge of a field and shooed away the oxen who continued the familiar road home. Stepan and I stealthily turned back toward the Kala[4] of Kessab, where I had seen Al Hawa. There we squatted down along a terrace wall and waited in the dark. A mere half an hour later in a nearby field, we noticed someone moving in our direction, crouching behind terrace walls. When he arrived to our hiding spot, all of a sudden both of us attacked him and bound his hands. We tied up his feet with the harness of the oxen that was with me and tied his mouth tightly with a headscarf so he wouldn't yell. Stepan-Ammo and I, dragged him like a dog (3 km, ed.) by his legs to satisfy our thirst for revenge, brought him home and tied him up well in one of the pens of the oxen. Later Stepan-Ammo and I sat down to decide what was the best location to make him disappear.

"While we were thinking what our next steps should be, we heard noises downstairs. We went to the barn with one of us standing guard outside. And what did we see? The thief, we don't know how, apparently with a small pocketknife he had hidden on him, had cut away the rope and was attempting to make a hole in the wall to flee. Immediately we restrained him and dragged him by the rope around his legs to the khanduog (dry water gorge, Kessab dialect[5]) that runs perpendicular to the Kessab road. We knew that in the khanduog there was quite a deep hole, like a well. It was a full moon at midnight. First, we sat him down and made him confess that he indeed was the horse thief.

"He bargained for life by promising he would compensate for his thievery by giving us his cash in addition a better horse than the one he had stolen. But I was so full of revenge that I picked a sharp-edged rock and

4 Kala means fortress in Arabic is a ruin of an ancient structure that has not been excavated. (Tcholakian [2015], p. 226).

5 In the Kessab dialect, *khanduog* is a deep narrow gorge with running water (sometimes dry), generally with rocky shoreline.

struck his head right below his ear. Thinking he was dead, we threw him in the pit that was two meters deep and began filling up the pit with stones. Fifteen minutes later we heard noises. So Stepan-Ammo cursing furiously went down the pit and completed the task. Together we filled the pit with boulders so that in the future no one would smell the stench of rotting flesh. Then having avenged, we returned home, without making anyone aware of what had happened."

Chapter 4
TO THE DESERT

Peaceful and constructive life in the village continued as usual until the First World War broke out. As call-to-arms mobilization began, Uncle Hovhannes and several eligible Manjikians were conscripted to the army while their mothers were wailing and crying. The village became discouraged with accumulating daily war reports. The village atmosphere became conspicuously ominous, especially when an unprecedented numbers of soldiers and policeman appeared throughout the Kessab region.

At the Karadouran seashore guardhouse the number of guards increased from the normal 2-3 to 25-30 *gendarmes* (soldiers).

Karadouran seashore today; At a distance Mousa Dagh (left), border of Syria and Turkey (right)

The villagers were horrified and saw dark clouds gathering all around. Rumor spread that the seashore population would be exiled.

This confusion lasted until the end of March 1915, when all of a sudden more than 150 gendarmes were sent to the region of Kessab. Thirty-five of them were sent to Karadouran. One day the parish leader of the Armenian Apostolic Church in Karadouran, Father Bedros Paboujian, came to our house, breathless and whispering to my father. In low tones he began a conversation, telling him about the exile. In the village Father Bedros and my father were well-known members of the Hnchak[1] party.

"My son, Minas, they are going to exile us to the deserts, so what are we waiting for? I will take the responsibility for poisoning 35 soldiers with rat poison. May God wrap my neck with that sin," Father Bedros said to my father. "So let's take the people immediately to Mt. Dounak (Mt. Dounak, which is unreachable and full of caves, is wedged in a forested mountain facing the village). You know, my son, if we take enough food with us to the mountain and seal off both of its entrances, we will be capable of defending ourselves for months against the army. My son, let's go to Kessab township and see what we can do about this."

They went to Kessab and consulted with the leaders of the other party, the Armenian Revolutionary Federation (ARF),[2] suggesting that it would be best to climb the mountain and defend themselves, as in Mousa Dagh, whose news of self-defense had already reached Kessab, rather than be driven into the deserts. The discussions did not yield any consensus. Armenian Catholics and Protestants[3] said the missionaries would defend them and that only the Armenian Apostolic Church members should be subject to exile. Therefore, the plan to defend did not materialize, and thus terror and despair prevailed among the people. And we, the children, were innocently surprised that our parents were so sad and anxious. Weren't we just going on a pleasant journey? We were interested and eager to see what would happen next.

A few days later at the end of July 1915, a town crier appeared and announced to the seashore community to get prepared to be relocated to the interior of the country,[4] away from the sea for a short time and

1 The Social Democratic Party, Hunchak means bell in Armenian, was formed in Jenev Switzerland in 1887

2 The ARF, founded 1890 in Tibilisi, Russian Empire, was also known as Tashnagsutyun in Armenian.

3 During the second half of the nineteenth century, through American and European missionaries the Evangelical and Catholic communities were formed.

4 Due to their experiences during the 1909 Adana Massacre, the locals had armed themselves. (See map page 45).

that the government would provide the necessary mules to take them away together with their belongings. Indeed a few days later, Turkish mule owners appeared in Karadouran and began to load the first caravan of about 400 people from the seashore. They left the beach area with sadness and sorrow.

In the following days more than 500 people from the Ghazarian, Manjikian, Kalemderian, and Kazazian families were forced to go into exile. The government provided a few more mules in addition to what we already had. My mom and dad did their best to take from home the necessary things which would make us comfortable, and at night they buried the rest of the copper plates and dishes in the yard. The lamenting adults and excited children kissed the door of our house before leaving it behind us. Instead of riding the mules, as our parents had insisted, we walked to Kessab. Only after leaving Kessab behind us were we so exhausted, so we naturally asked to ride the mules.

Our caravan, which was controlled by several gendarmes, crossed mountains and valleys in a long file. The first village that we came to was our neighboring Turkish village of Ordou. The inhabitants shouted with malice and so-called compassion the names of those whom they recognized bidding, "*Oughurlar olsun*" (Good luck, farewell), hopefully you will return soon," etc. These very same residents who bid us a safe return, along with other Turkish villagers, ransacked our homes and belongings immediately after we passed them by. I will amplify details of this episode later in my story.

Near a village far from Ordou, where there was a spring, I do not recall the name, we spent our first night in exile. The people were exhausted. They put the loads down and started fires, and each family prepared a separate dinner, as if at home. Immediately after dinner we, the children, who had been so excited to leave our homes, now tired, laid down on the ground and fell into their usual deep sleep.

Here we noticed one of my uncles, Garabet, who was a member of the ARF party, had disappeared, leaving us all in grief. My uncle did not wish to be exiled, and so he fled and returned to Kessab. I will tell you about this later.

Our first morning the gendarmes woke us up before sunrise. Under their orders and threats to be quick, we immediately stacked our mules,

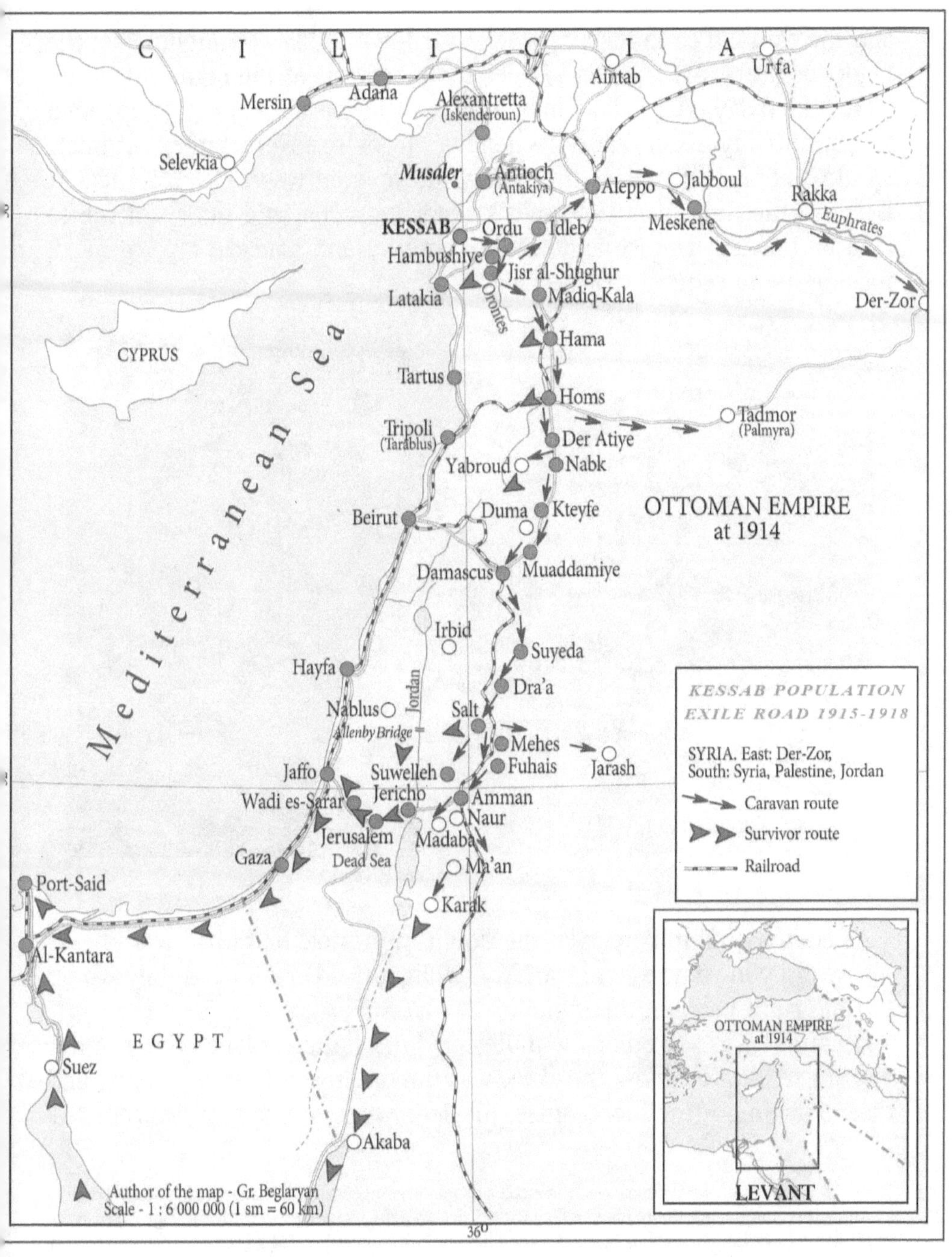

Kevork's WWI Odyssey, 1915-1920 (Caravan Route)

and the caravan continued its way to the town of Jisr al-Shughur,[5] on the banks of the Orontes River, where the people spent the night.

Our third day is especially memorable for me because of what happened to me and my sister Zabel. Whenever I got tired my father or uncle would put me on one of the mules; the owner was a Turk muleteer. Because the mule was fully overloaded, its owner did not want me to ride or burden it more and would come by and squeeze my leg hard, forcing me to request that he take me down.

Jisr al-Shughur Orontes River

As soon as the muleteer let me down, my uncle or father would ask, "Why did you come down, son? You will get tired again," and they would put me right back on the mule.

Because I was scared of the muleteer, I did not complain, so my father and uncle did not know the Turk was hurting me. After embarking and disembarking a few more times, my legs were completely bruised. My

5 Jisr al-Shughur, in the Orontes Valley, served as a major refugee camp for Armenians deported from Antioch region during the Armenian Genocide. Turkish gendarmes forced caravans southward, with groups sent to Hama, Aleppo, Meskene, and Der Zor, where many faced atrocities. One group from Kessab was split: some perished in Der Zor, while others remained temporarily in Jisr al-Shughur.. (see map on p.45)

uncle wanted to put me back on the mule. I declined to be put back, crying. When he insisted to know the reason for declining to mount the mule I said, "Look, my skin is blue from the muleteer's painful pinches."

My senior uncle, Zenop, who was the toughest and strongest man in the village, seeing my bruised condition, lost his mind. Enraged, he attacked and strangled the muleteer so hard that his tongue was hanging out from his mouth.

Three or four people, including my father and other uncles, were barely able to save the man, who was half-dead as he lay prostrate on the ground. The gendarmes broke up the fight. When they realized what had happened, they did not say anything to Uncle Zenop, but profusely cursed him. However, they got angry at the mule owner, shouting that if he hurt me again, they would punish him. The incident ended without my uncle getting into any trouble with the soldiers.

That same day near the Sunni village of Madiq-kala (Qalaat al-Madiq), which lies between Jisr al-Shughur and Hama, horse-riding Bedouins appeared and advised my mother to hand over my little sister Zabel, who was two years old and a beautiful child, explaining that Turks planned to kill us all. Naturally, my mother refused. However, after walking for more than a kilometer, those same Bedouins reappeared and successfully whisked away Zabel and escaped. Uncle Zenop immediately dropped the load from one of the mules, mounted the mule and began a chase after them. Two soldiers joined him. As the pursuit continued, the Bedouins realized that the military was chasing them too, they placed Zabel on the ground and disappeared in the nearby hills. My uncle, with my sister in his arms, caught up with the caravan on the mule; he handed my sister back to my mom, who was wailing and sobbing along with us the whole time. That third night we rested near Lake Madiq-kala. For days and weeks, we walked until we reached Hama City.

The sale of all those animals did not affect my childhood imagination as much as the sale of our family cow, Jeyran, who provided us with dairy nutrition.

It was a beautiful reddish cow with a diamond-shaped patch of white hair on its forehead. She was a clever animal, whose calf followed her. Before milking the cow, I would stroke the diamond-shaped patch of hair, and it would lick my hands like she would lick her calf, with a pleading look. And sometimes I would also sit under it to suckle the milk from its udder. I wanted to be safe and see if it would kick. It never did.

So the family decided to sell our dear Jeyran, but they kept that decision to themselves because it was inevitable that we would start crying. Finally, an Arab man started bargaining with my father, came to an agreement, paid for the cow, and took it away. My brothers and I started crying. The scene was heartbreaking. When the buyer walked away, pulling Jeyran behind him, Jeyran looked back, teary-eyed, and started mooing, as if asking us, "Why are you handing me and my calf over to a stranger?"

Seeing how the animal reacted intelligently to this situation, tears welled up in my parents' eyes as well. This way all our livestock were sold in Hama, except for the mules, which we needed to reach Homs. They, too, were sold in Homs. Our entire caravan now became a camel caravan and transported us from Homs to Damascus,[6] Syria.

We stayed in the parks of Damascus for a while. After that the soldiers packed us onto the railroad freight cars to the city of Amman,[7] Jordan. For months the exiled refugees either camped outdoors or in the ancient caves of the partly ruined Amman Amphitheatre until they were gradually settled in different Jordanian villages.

6 Damascus is the capital of Syria. Some 130,000 Armenian deportees were driven there.

7 The inhabitants of Karadouran and Bashord arrived in Jordan and lived there as refugees for three years. They scattered to different villages (like Wadi es-Sarar, Gjes, Remmen, Mehes, Remenin, and Salt) in Jordan to find employment and living facilities. Quite a few families sought refuge near Amman and the people from Karadouran renamed it Magharinen (meaning "the caves"). It was an ancient suburb of Suediya. Still others took shelter with Christian families in the village Salt. Others reached Ma'an. The refugees sowed, harvested, farmed, constructed roads and worked in construction. For the entire month and seven days from Kessab to Amman, Father Bedros never separated from his parishioners. Remembered for his courage, he married many couples on the Hama-Damascus Road and provided them with an escape route to Jordan. For about three years, while in Jordan, he married couples, supervised them, got them jobs, and provided them with assistants. (Tcholakian, H. [2004]. Kessab. Vol. 3 (p. 494). The Studies Union of Kessabtsies Living in America)

Hama

The city of Homs, Syria, pre-WW-I

Damascus, the capital of Syria, pre-WW-I

My grandfather and his family first settled under an oak tree in a park of a Christian village owned by Bedouins called Fuhais. The scene was unbelievable because a family of about 20 were all sheltered together under the shade of one tree, outdoors in that autumn weather. Other families had the same fate in the parks until the government housed us all.

Amman, the capital of Jordan, 1952

Chapter 5
DEATH AND BIRTH

A month later, in October 1915, my father, Uncle Zenop, Uncle Hovhannes' wife, and her son settled in a room in a Muslim Bedouin village called Mehes. (Uncle Hovhannes was a conscripted soldier in the Turkish Army at that time). The government had forcibly seized the room that they settled in from its landlord, Abu Musa al-Madi. The owner's wife had passed away. They had only a son named Musa. Abu Musa al-Madi's sister, Khazna, who was unmarried and blind in one eye, was responsible for the well-being of the family and the house.

Kevork's mother Yeghisapet Kairchian Manjikian.

Our family's 14 members with all our belongings settled in a 4 x 5-meter room, which left no space to move around. During those long months of travel from Kessab to Jordan, the people's financial and material resources had vanished. As a result, all the men immediately began to work on road constructions. My father, like the others, would go far from the village to cut stones for the construction of the roads.

At that time, due to the large number of lice found among the military, the epidemic known as typhus had spread, which was something normal among the Bedouins. The people of our village also got infected, and many died because of the lack of medicine or doctors. Thus, in a few months, more than 50 Manjikians died of typhus. Among them were my grandfather and grandmother, my youngest uncle, Avedis, Uncle Zenop's wife and eldest daughter, Dzaghganush, and my soldier-uncle Hovhannes' wife and their only child, Dikran. My father was also a victim.

I would like to describe here the circumstances of my father's death, which have been imprinted in my childhood memory. I must say that my father was a God-fearing and church-loving man, and he had even wanted to be ordained a priest, but because my mother refused to be the wife of a priest, he didn't fulfill his dream. One day after returning from road construction (rock crushing) work, my father looked tired and sad and laid down. It was clear that he also had the typhus. For days, my father lay ill in bed. My mother, with tears in her eyes, provided all she could under the circumstances. My father would become delirious and would have nightmares from time to time. I, being mischievous, did not hesitate to steal and eat the dry *kaak* (breakfast biscuit) that my mother had put aside for my father.

My mother got angry and said, "Don't you see your father is dying? Aren't you ashamed you are eating his share of bread…?"

Then my father opened his eyes and with an emotional tone told my mother, "Yeghis, there is no need to rebuke him. I am unable to eat anything, let him be." Before this, I had never seen my father as kind as he was that day.

At the time of my father's illness, my mother was already pregnant[1] and about to give birth. One day my father unexpectedly asked, "Yeghsa, what did you name the new little one?"

My mother started crying, saying that the baby was not born yet. It became obvious that my father was delirious.

One sunny morning in February 1916, my father seemed to feel better

1 Kevork's mother Yeghisapet (or Yeghsapet) was at least 2 months pregnant when the deportation began.

and, after drinking his milk in the morning, asked my mother to bring the big family Bible. On the last page of the Bible, the dates of marriages, births, or deaths of our family were recorded, and he wanted to read a page from it to us, but he was unable. When he saw that he couldn't, he asked his first-born, my older brother Hovsep, 13 years old, to open the Bible and read one of the pages. It turned out that Hovsep opened the Bible to a page where Christ tells his students, "Just as the birds in the sky do not worry about their livelihood, so you should not worry about anything."[2]

When my brother finished reading, my father, who had noticed my mother's weeping said, "Yeghsa, didn't you hear what the Bible said? You do not have to worry about anything. Just as God cares for birds, He will care for His creatures and orphans, too." At that instant, it seemed that he felt that the end was near, and we were going to be orphaned.

Half an hour had barely passed when we heard our mother's screaming, so we rushed in and saw that my father, with a smile on his face, had passed away. From that day, we became orphans.

Our father, without a coffin, was buried in the Armenian cemetery, which was set aside by the government for Armenians in the village of Mehes. My uncles and relatives dug the ground, made it the shape of a coffin, and put my father there to rest. They then covered it with flat stones and earth. Father Bedros Paboujian of Karadouran, who was from the same political party as my father, recited the requiem prayers for his soul. With heavy hearts, we clung to my mother's skirts and returned home.

On the seventh day of my father passing away, my mother gave birth to a girl. We had no more means to live by. So about 40 days after childbirth, my mother would go early in the mornings to the woods, which was about an hour away from the village of Mehes, chop wood, and bring it home on her back. She would then make a meal for us. Thereafter she would carry the bundle of wood on her back to the city of Salt, which was about two hours' walk from our village. She would sell the bundle for a few coins or for some flour or wheat. This would continue every God-given day.

2 Matthew 6.26: "Look at the birds in the sky: they neither sow nor reap nor gather into barns, and yet your heavenly Father feeds them. Are you not of more value than they?"

One morning in March, we went together. However, because it was too cold, I could no longer walk with her despite her promises that she would get acorns for me. Therefore, crying and screaming, I sat under a bush, and my mother went into the forest to gather her daily bundle of firewood. Suddenly, a Circassian[3] horseman passing by noticed me, approached me, and questioned me in Turkish. Out of fear I could not speak, even though I did not understand Turkish anyway. But he dismounted, gathered some firewood, lit a fire for me, and left. From afar my mother witnessed what had happened, came after the man left, and she warmed herself as well. I forgot all my fears when I saw she really kept her promise and had the acorns, which we roasted and ate. Finally, my mother and I walked back to the village.

3 The *Circassian* were originally a Christian people living in eastern Crimea. In the 17th century, many converted to Islam. Later, during the 19th century, they were driven out by the Russians and relocated to western Armenia. Subsequently, most of them migrated to Transjordan in the early 19th century.

Chapter 6
THE ORPHANAGE

One day a few months after my father's death Grandpa Mateos, one of my grandfather's younger brothers, came to us and informed my mother that he wanted to take several orphans to the German orphanage in Jerusalem, and asked my mother if she would like to send me to an orphanage.

My mother turned to me and asked, "Son, do you want Grandpa Mateos to take you to a boarding school?"

German Schneller Orphanage, Jerusalem.

I did not understand what an orphanage was then. It was a novelty for a boy my age to be sent far away to a school. I gladly accepted. On the other hand, my uncles insisted that I should not be sent away. Grandfather Mateos made an appointment and asked me to be ready in a week so that he could come from Salt and take me with him to Jerusalem.

I spent a lot of time in our village gardens, mischief-making, stealing vegetables. My naughtiness was torturing poor Khazna's soul, the landlord's sister. I had learned Arabic curses that Khazna generously used on me ... on the other hand, the landlord's son, Musa, a kind young man around 19-20 years old, always took care of me and spoiled me. It must be said that throughout this exile, this very kind family treated my mother and her children with considerable goodness. I will talk about them in the next pages.

Jordan River Valley

A week later on a Sunday, Grandfather Mateos came and took me to their home in Salt. Early the following morning we headed to Jerusalem. We were seven orphans, all from Karadouran. We had to take turns riding the only donkey that my Grandfather Mateos had. I think the day was in April in 1916. The first hour walking down the Salt Valley was pleasant. And when we came to the Jordan River Valley, a place called Ghor, it was annoyingly hot. At times riding on the donkey, taking turns, and sometimes on foot, we reached the Jordan River wooden bridge, later renamed the Allenby Bridge,[1] and crossed it.

We came to the city of Jericho, where we spent the night on the bare floor in a khan. The room had only a fire burning. After a bread and

1 In 1885, the Ottoman government constructed a wooden bridge across the River Jordan near Jericho. In 1918, British general Edmond Allenby built a bridge in the original location which has since become known as the Allenby Bridge.

halva (sweet crumbly sesame candy) for dinner, we laid down on the floor, using the small bundle of our clothes as a pillow. Naturally for the first time, I missed my mother's care and hugs. Let me remind you that at the time the *zeboon* (men's long village tunic) wrapped around the waist with an Aleppo belt and *yemenis* (covered slippers) for shoes were the local costume of the village boys.

The Allenby Bridge at the Jordan-Palestine border

Early on Tuesday morning we resumed our uphill climb to Jerusalem, which was tiring for us, the children. We, the seven orphans, continued on our way, sometimes walking, at times riding on the donkey until we reached Jerusalem, and took shelter in the Armenian monastery of St. James. It seems that Grandfather Mateos had previously made arrangements for our stay. The next day he handed us over to the director of the German Schneller Orphanage.[2] Grandfather Mateos kissed each of us and wept as he parted from us. Unfortunately, I never saw him again because he also died in Salt in his exile.

The five of us who were over 12 years old were taken to the adult part of the orphanage, while I and another boy who were barely 11, were handed over to Nun Ida's children's section of the orphanage. They immediately took us to the bath, shaved our hair to baldness, and put

2 German Protestant orphanage, Jerusalem from 1860 to 1940.

shorts on us that had a doublet above with two to three buttons on the back. We were made to wear high-heeled shoes that seemed strange to us. All the children were Arabs, of course, and we didn't know Arabic, except for a few curses inherited from Khazna. An hour later I wanted to go to the bathroom, but I did not know how to unbutton those useless buttons. I almost had to do it in my shorts ... so I started crying. When Aunt Ida asked me why I was crying, I somehow made her understand that I had a natural need to do and could not get out of the clothing, so she taught me the way.

Panoramic view of Jerusalem, pre-WW-I

Because I didn't know Arabic and couldn't play with the other boys, I felt very sad and stayed away for a few days. It must be noted that the kindergarten section of that Schneller Orphanage was a beautiful clean place and had a yard full of toys. There was particularly a carousel, like a big spinning top where five to six boys could sit and spin. However, lacking confidence, I did not dare go near it.

A few days later, frustrated and conflicted, I would not join the others. As I just watched them play with that huge spinning top, one of the boys from Lifta, a village near Jerusalem, approached me and said, "*Ta'al nil'aab*," which means "Let's play." Since I only knew swear words in Arabic, I thought that he was cursing me saying, "*I'll'aan*," which is a curse.

Because of a troublesome sentiment, which I had bottled up for days, I kicked the boy so hard that a few boys were barely able to save him. As anticipated, I also started crying aloud, calling out "*Mayrig*" (mother) in Armenian. Soon the supervisor, Aunt Ida, came, but I couldn't explain to her why I had beaten the boy up. I kept repeating in Armenian that how dare he curse at me saying, "I'll'aan," and I went on crying. Desperate, they brought in a boy from the older boys' section named Karnig Dakessian, who knew a little Armenian, to find out why I had beaten up Dib. I explained that he had cursed at me saying, "I'll'aan."

The boy was asked to repeat what he had said to me and when he said, "Ta'al nil'aab," I confirmed that was what Dib had said.

Karnig then explained to me that Dib wanted to do me a favor and play with me, as *Ta'al nil'aab* means "Let's play."

After apologizing to Dib, I became that boy's best friend. In spite of being beaten up wrongfully, this fine boy began to play with me and gradually taught me to speak Arabic. And so, a few months later, I started speaking enough Arabic and German.

The Schneller Orphanage ran very smoothly. Our section included 60 orphans between the ages of 8 and 11. In a huge bedroom, each orphan had his own bed, covered with clean sheets and blankets with a red top, all identical and clean. In the morning as soon as the bell rang, we would each run downstairs to wash. Each of us was assigned our own wash basin and towel. After washing we would head to the dining hall.

Due to war, food was scarce and tasteless. In the morning our breakfast was a piece of bread and a glass of boiled, roasted, and ground barley water, like boiled tea but without sugar. At our age when children needed nutrition to grow up, we were given very small slices of bread that disappeared after two bites. Lunch was generally a soup of grain or rice with cooked vegetable leaves and a slice of bread. And supper was one piece of bread with four to five olives or a piece of bread with 5-10 dried figs or a handful of raisins.

When I was in the orphanage, I always felt hungry. We were given food just so we could stay alive. One day a week we had a piece of meat in the soup or in the rice, and the rest of the days there was no meat. We waited impatiently for Christmas and New Year, because we would enjoy big slices of pastry, like cakes with raisins and two thick peel Jaffa[3] oranges. Those were the only few days of the year when we would eat well. Because we craved food, we would eat the orange peel first and then the fruit itself so we could fill up our stomachs.

Despite the lack of nutrition, our clothes were very nice and tidy; the linens were neat and clean; and we were given a bath every week. From a health point of view, this was great. Our studies lasted only half a day, from 8 in the morning 'til 12 noon. And in the afternoon, after 2:30 p.m., the little ones were taken to the *adzou* (vegetable gardens). Whenever we were lucky enough to put a veggie leaf in our mouths, even though covered with earth, we would chew it quickly and swallow it.

Jaffa, a major seaport in Palestine 1917-1918

3 Jaffa, or Yaffa, is a port city on the Mediterranean renowned for its oranges, the best on the Mediterranean coast.

Some of the older boys were taken to the fields to work, and others did artisanship. The German Schneller Orphanage had large fields, gardens, and orchards that provided its annual food supply. In the summer, it was pleasant to see the older students go to the field to reap the harvest. We looked forward to growing up and following in their footsteps.

And so life continued in this way until the winter of 1917, when the war front came nearer to Jerusalem, and even General Allenby's bombs began to fall in the vicinity of our orphanage. By that time, I had already been moved to the older boys' section, and my guardian was 17-year-old brave Karnig Dakessian. He was my protector in every way, and woe to the boy who in some way harassed me or fought with me. Karnig would immediately come and beat him up.

One night the bombing intensified so much that we were ordered to go to the shelters located on the ground floor. Karnig, taking two other boys from our village with him said, "Come on, I know a good place to stay." At that time, Karnig, who would bring food to the teachers from the cellars, was the lead-off person of the cellars. I do not know how he had managed to steal a big loaf of bread, weighing almost two kilos, and hid it discreetly under his arm. During those bombings, he sneaked us into the cellar and locked the door. We were overjoyed; in the huge cellar there was wine in barrels, dried figs and raisins in sacks, olives, and especially a huge loaf of bread that could last us for a few days. Karnig offered us generous portions of bread and added that we were welcome to eat whatever we desired in the cellar.

Without waiting for the invitation to be repeated, we started eating all kinds of food like hungry wolves. A little further ahead we saw Karnig drinking from a straw he had inserted into a barrel. Answering our question, he said that it was wine and that if we wished, we could, too. I had never drunk wine before. So out of curiosity I started drinking from the rubber tube. It had a pleasant, sweet taste — aged wine — so assuming it was some kind of juice, I drank a little more as did the others. Less than an hour later, we were all completely drunk and immediately fell into a deep slumber.

The next morning when the bombings stopped, while the teachers were assembling the students, they noticed that we were not there. After looking for us everywhere, when they were looking through the cellar window, they found us sleeping. They started bashing on the door.

Partially drunk, Karnig opened the door, and the three of us hadn't even heard the commotion. All of a sudden, we found ourselves in the beds of the orphanage hospital. When we finally came to our senses the school superintendent, as punishment, whipped us five times.

After that the day went by peacefully, and it snowed at night. Early the next morning there was pandemonium in the school: the British had entered Jerusalem and captured it. A few Armenian boys ran away from school to greet the British Army. And indeed, after making sure they were English, Karnig, without skipping a heartbeat, climbed the school bell tower, lowered the German and Turkish flags, and raised the British flag (I don't know how he had got hold of it), turning a blind eye to the belligerent glances coming from the German teachers and the superintendent. That boy's alienated Armenian blood boiled, as if to take revenge for the Armenians.

Gen. Allenby approachin Jaffa Gate, 1917

At about 10 a.m., the vanguards of the British Army were spotted. Some of them were stationed in the gardens and fields around the Schneller Orphanage. Two days later, after gathering all the Turkish and German teachers and taking them away, the British took over the school themselves. At first chance after the takeover of the school by the British, our stomachs were full. We had plenty of bread, biscuits, canned meat and food, and we also had meat dishes. A week later, they started teaching us English, which we comprehended very easily since it seemed to be close to the German language. And so our nourishment also became enhanced.

Gen. Allenby entering Jerusalem through Jaffa Gate, 11 December, 1917

Chapter 7
THE FAMILY IN EXILE

Barely two months after these events the British Army also retreated northeast to Jordan and occupied Transjordan, but only a week later they retreated back to Jerusalem during the winter of 1917.

General Allenby entering Damascus, October 1918

The exiled Armenian families, taking this opportunity, fled to Jerusalem with the British Army retreat. Among them were my mother, my younger brother, Nishan, my sisters, Sarah and Zabel, who were living at the time in my uncle's house in Salt. The people took whatever they could carry and fled to Jerusalem, arriving there in February 1918. In the orphanage I was completely cut off from my mother, sisters, and brother and had no news from them for a long time (1916 to 1918).

When I heard that some exiled Armenians were settling inside the Turkish military barracks next to the St. James Monastery, I at once and without anyone knowing ditched out of the school compound and went seeking out my family in that Turkish barracks

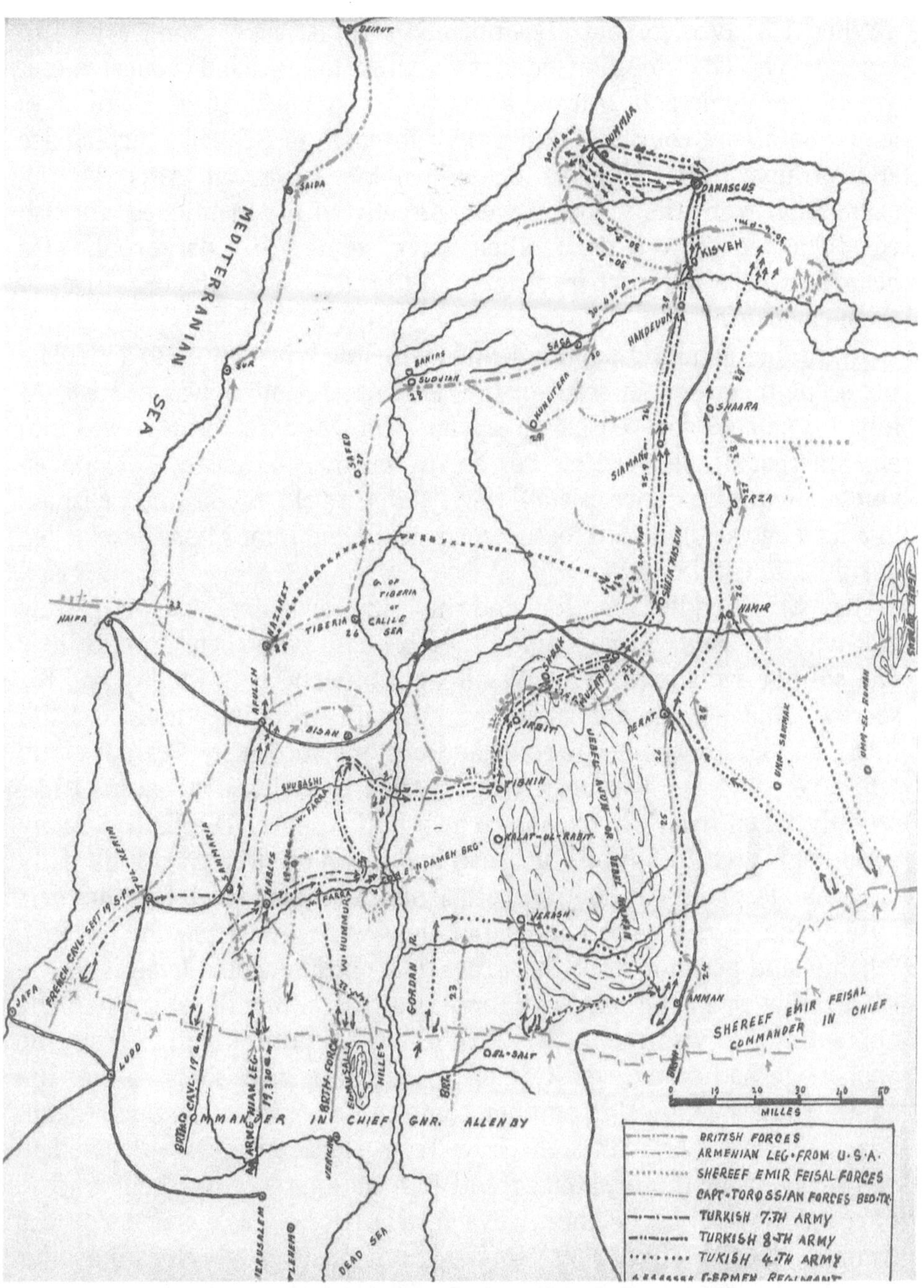

Captain Torossian's map of General Allenby's decisive battle from Jerusalem to Damascus.
The Ottoman Empire surrendered to the Allies a month after this victory.

When I arrived, organizers informed me that they would arrive in several days. Therefore, I handed my address to them and requested that my mother come and visit me at school when she arrived. A few days later one of my cousins found a way to come to Schneller orphanage and brought me the news of my mother's arrival. After getting permission from the school, I went directly to the mentioned Turkish barracks, seeking out my mother. They pointed to a dark room at a distance where my mother, sisters, and brother were staying. I ran to them eagerly.

My mother and I were overwhelmed with joy. When I want to articulate the scene of misery in front of me, I tremble. Mother was in rags. At least 60 patches covered her dress, and she was barefoot. She was thin and unrecognizable. The clothes on my brother and sisters were even worse, their appearance as well. Barely 11 years old, my brother, Nishan, in a torn *zeboon* and bare feet seemed sickly and thin. My sisters looked healthier but still in rags.

They were huddled, barefoot and shivering, on a dirty worn-out straw mat with the only village blanket they brought with them around their feet so they wouldn't freeze. We all wept bitterly, both for joy and for sorrow. And my mother showered me with unending kisses as I did them. I asked my brother to come and visit me once every few days, and whenever he came, I would give him dried figs, olives, or raisins I had secretly taken from my friends to help him recover. The British Army would also give 750 grams of bread and a can of sweetened milk daily to each exile. This was their and other migrants' only food. Despite their misery the people were happy that they were free from the Turkish "chains" and began to hope that from now on they would live....

They stayed in the barracks for more than a month, and I had the opportunity to visit them several times. My beautiful clothes from the orphanage had made everyone envious. There were rumors that the exiles would be moved to another camp in Port Said, near Suez Canal, Egypt. So together with some boys from Karadouran, we decided to run away from the orphanage and join our parents on their way to Port Said. My older brother, Hovsep, who worked as a shepherd near Amman for the Circassians, stayed there (instead of retreating with the British). We had heard no news of him, and my mother lamented his absence.

When we confirmed their departure date to Port Said, one night underneath our beautiful Sunday clothes, we wore our everyday clothes and ran away from the orphanage with Karnig's help and joined our parents. The following morning, they came from the orphanage to look for us, but in that large crowd it was easy to hide so that we could not be noticed. My mother, considering our misery, tried hard to convince me to stay in the orphanage and not to accompany her, but all of her advice was in vain.

A week before Easter in 1918, our caravan headed to the train station in Jerusalem. When we were passing by the St. James Monastery, we saw that the Armenian General Benevolent Union (AGBU) was handing out clothing to the needy. I begged the priest in charge to give my mother one of the handouts to cover her, but my plea fell on deaf ears — it seemed that the clothing was reserved for the neediest people. I was able to restrain myself from showering the *vartapet* (priest of the Armenian Apostolic Church) with a thousand curses. I swore to myself that I would find work as a child laborer in order to earn money to cover the nakedness of my mother, brother, and two sisters.

The exiled population was loaded onto railroad freight cars, and five to six stations away from Jerusalem, we settled in a tent city on the outskirts of a railroad station called Wadi es-Sarar, which was directly under the auspices of the British Army. The folks stayed there for more than four months. It was in that tent city of Wadi es-Sarar that we reunited with the surviving Manjikians. It turned out that during exile in Palestine and Jordan, approximately 70 Manjikians perished, including my grandfather's brothers, except for the eldest brother, Yessayi,[1] about whom I would like to say a few words since he had an interesting past as senior authority of the Manjikians and as their leader.

1 Third generation Manjikian, Yessayi known as Aysa Manjik Agha, was the elder of his generation. When the announcement of Young Turk Revolution was in effect in 1908, Turk government officials, neighboring Turkish villagers, Alawite Arab villagers, Greek villagers, came to Kessab township. They celebrated with speeches, music and dance. During the festivities, the skeptical Aysa Manjik Agha reportedly said, **"Let's wait and see on whose head this noise making revolution will explode."** (Tcholakian [1995], p. 89).

The Monument at Rafat-Arara, Palestine (moved to Mount Zion, Israel, 1925), dedicated to Armenian fallen heroes who fought with General Allenby, 1918

Grandfather Yessayi was the *agha* (leader) of the village of Karadouran at a young age as well as the *moukhtar* (village mayor) and a fierce opponent of Protestantism. The aghas of the neighboring Turkish villagers treated him with respect. As my memory would serve me correctly, Grandfather Yessayi spend his daytime hours underneath his giant pear tree, facing the street, greeting all the passers-by.

One day, when one of the Protestant *patveli* (preacher, honorable one) was returning from Karadouran seashore riding a mule, as he went by the courtyard, Grandfather Yessayi (to subtly express that the preacher was blind to the insincerity of the people he was converting) gave the preacher a *mouyokhr* (cedar wood, which is as flammable as a candle and has an aromatic scent), handed it to him, and said, "Please, take it."

The preacher asked, "What is this, Yessayi Agha?"

Grandfather Yessayi said, "So that during daytime you can recruit for followers of the Protestant faith." He wanted to say that insensitive and incorrigible people were in their midst.

On another occasion one of our Manjikian girls got engaged to a

Protestant man. When this man with his guests visited the girl's house in Karadouran, it was customary to sing *ilahi* (spiritual songs). One night when such songs were being sung, Grandfather Yessayi took the opportunity and asked his younger son to take the hide of a newly stripped donkey to the house, where the ilahi was being performed and to tell them, "Since you are in mourning, my father suggested that you should also mourn this donkey's hide."[2]

Grandfather Yessayi was also the terror of the village brides. Woe to any housewife or any girl who walked by without kissing his hand. I have seen an incident with my own eyes when my mother ran across the elderly leader, Grandfather Yessayi, in the street near our house. My mother took Yessayi's extended hand and kissed it. However, it looked instead as if she had only brought his hand to her forehead. Immediately, Yessayi grabbed my mother's hand, giving it an exaggerated demonstration of a kiss and said, "This is how it is done." My mother was left embarrassed and ashamed.

Grandfather Yessayi had a daily habit of downing a shot of *araq* (anise-flavored liqueur, Arabic; *ouzo,* Greek). When he visited a Manjikian hearth, the family would automatically serve him a small glass of araq. If he liked it he would say, "Your araq is good, but your measure is small," making them understand that he wanted a second serving.

When mothers wanted to restrain their children's misbehavior, they told them, "If you are naughty, I will complain to Grandfather Yessayi."

He was so charismatic, we calmed down. But in reality he was a very simple, kind, senior elderly authority and a modest and honest man, who adored children very much.

It was customary that Turkish or Armenian mayors with their entourage would exchange visits as part of a good-neighbor policy. One day Ahmad Agha, the mayor of the Turkish village of Bedrusiye, together with his entourage visited our Grandfather Yessayi. In those days Grandfather Yessayi was a renowned hunter. He not only had the best hunting weapons but also possessed acclaimed hunting dogs. Ahmad

2 People were familiar with Armenian Apostolic Church hymns and melodies, but Protestant hymns were foreign to their ears. While Protestants sang hymns during festive occasions, their hymns sounded mournful. Yessayi wanted to mock these mournful hymns as inappropriate for an upcoming wedding celebration. So, he wryly suggested they mourn something appropriate, like recently deceased donkey's hide.

Agha, upon seeing one of the puppies, asked Yessayi for a gift puppy. Grandfather Yessayi willingly gave the puppy to him. Then the Agha and his entourage, along with the puppy, left. Months later Grandfather Yessayi and his entourage reciprocated by visiting Ahmad Agha in the Turkish village of Bedrusiye. During the meal the puppy that was given as a gift entered, now all grown up.

Ahmad Agha exclaimed, "Osht, Manjik," at the puppy and shooed him out of the room.

At once Grandfather Yessayi realized that the dog's name, on purpose or not, was his namesake — the shortened version of his family name, Manjik. My grandfather turned red but managed not to show it and waited for the opportune moment to teach Ahmad Agha a lesson. Months thereafter Ahmad Agha riding his mule and with his men visited my grandfather. Grandfather Yessayi, with his eldest son, Hovsep, welcomed the guests into his courtyard.

After greeting them properly in Turkish, pointed to the mule and asked his son in a loud voice and in Turkish, "Hovsep, my son, tie Ahmad Agha in the barn and feed him the best barley."

Ahmad Agha became enraged and said, "How dare you label my mule with my name?"

My grandfather answered in return, "With the same audacity that you had named the hunting puppy by my name, Manjik."

Ahmad Agha accepted his mistake, apologized, and said that it was unintentional. Instead of entering the house and having some food or being entertained, he and his men returned to their village, a walking distance of about two hours. He killed the dog and on the same day took its carcass back to my Grandfather Yessayi's house and said, "See, the controversy between us will be put to an end this way. Only now I accept your hospitality." The oldest of his siblings, my grandfather's reputation was so big that even the government officials of those times respected him.

When I heard that our elder leader Grandfather Yessayi was alive, I wanted to see him at all costs. After making lentil soup, my mother asked us to take it to father and ask him to say a prayer for us. Nishan, my younger brother, and I took the soup and went to Grandfather's tent, where we found him laying down. He must have been 90 years old then. His hearing and vision were impaired a little. After we exchanged greeting, he wanted to know who our father was. After recognizing us, the good old man recalled the details of our father's passing. He blessed us and asked us to leave the soup with him and be on our way. Two days after our visit, Yessayi, the last one of our grandfathers, passed away under miserably humiliating conditions and so far away from his heavenly birthplace. Everyone said that Grandfather Yessayi could have lived for 10 more years if he had his share of the araq....

Let me add that Grandfather Yessayi was a God-fearing elderly senior, a devout follower of Armenian Apostolic Church, and a true believer and upholder of our ancestral church and family traditions and customs in all their ancient detailed rituals. I could never forget his special corner in church for Sunday mass. There he knelt from the start to the end of the divine liturgy, make the sign of the cross and continually praying. It was not obvious for whom he was praying for such a long time. As my mother explained, every time he made the sign of the cross, he would recite a prayer for one son, grandson, great-grandson. At the end of Divine Liturgy, he would reverently fold the square pillow cushion on which he knelt and store it in the cupboard next to it. He would not leave the church without kissing the Holy Bible in the priest's hand. Outside in the church courtyard he would greet everyone, ask about their well beings, give a piece of advice to one, and berate another. Only then would he return home.

Wadi es-Sarar, Jordan

In Wadi es-Sarar, we were given a tent, in which we placed our things: an old rug, one blanket for all six of us, a copper pot, a pan, one large copper plate, a few wooden spoons, and second-hand clothing for my mother, brother, and sisters. I had my Sunday outfit from the orphanage, my everyday clothes, a pair of shoes that were in good conditions still.

Seeing my mother, brother, and sisters' rags and exposed bodies, broke my heart. I yearned to find any kind of work immediately so that I would be able to replace their rags with proper clothing. I couldn't find the courage to ask my mother about their two years of hardship, leaving that for another time. I had promised myself not to open their wounds of misery unless I first got them the badly needed clothes; covering their feet was secondary.

Three days after settling down in the tent city, my brother and I went to the Wadi es-Sarar station, an hour's walk from where we stayed. This Indian military base was at the outskirts of the Wadi es-Sarar railroad station and at a further distance of half an hour south was the British military base. Despite our young age — I being 13, my brother 11 — and despite the foreign appearance of the Indian soldiers, I had the courage to approach their guard. In broken English, which I had learned at the Schneller Orphanage during the month and a half I had lived under British authority, tried to make the guard understand that I would like to have permission to enter the camp to look for any kind of service work there for my brother and me.

Clearly the Indian guard carefully inspected our appearance and noted the difference in my neatly dressed and my brother's unkempt appearance and, perhaps remembering his own children, took pity on us and pointed to the corner of the building where the kitchen and canteen area of the base were, shouting orders in Hindu, "Give them food," I think. Immediately the cook gave us some food. After eating some, I begged him to give us a service job to do in exchange for money, with which I could get some clothes for my brother, mother, and sisters. This was my only worry. That same day, he kept us busy around the kitchen. At times the soldiers would tell me to go to the canteen to get them some cigarettes or drinks and let me keep the change as a favor.

Later that day I had earned about 10 Egyptian *piasters* (cents). In the evening, before returning home, they presented us with a box filled with meat, bread, toast, and most importantly, a slightly worn woolen military uniform. We returned to the tent promptly in high spirits. My mother was anxiously waiting for us. The poor woman was worried, saying, "All day hungry and thirsty, where have you been?" We related to her our success story. My mother was ecstatic, particularly with the old military uniform we had brought back with us. She at once began to do some alterations to the uniform that transformed it into a pair of pants and a jacket for my brother.

She sewed under the dim light of an oil lamp 'til midnight. When she got up the next morning, she dressed my brother with warmth and joy. It could be funny to imagine changing a grown-up man's woolen uniform into an 11-year-old boy's clothing sewn hurriedly by hand, an absolute need. This awkward but effective hand-sewn reduction gave great satisfaction to my mother and me. For my mother, not having seen a coin during the past years, now had 10 Egyptian piasters. Although an insignificant amount, that could buy us a lot of things.

Inspired from the latest turn of events my brother and I worked for several weeks in the Indian Base. My brother was looking as smart as I and was not shivering from the cold of being half naked. We would return home every day with 10 piasters and a box of food. Let me mention that the exiled ones were given food once a day, generally something like a thick soup with either lentil or rice, at times with meat, and a lot of bread. In the evenings, we were served meat in tins. Thus, the box of food we brought home from the base was additional nourishment for my mother and the emaciated bodies of my sisters and brother.

After a few weeks, an Indian Captain advised us to go to the nearby British base, where we could even earn more money. He handed us a note to give to his friend, a British corporal. We showed the note to the guard who smiled, started to talk to me in English, and smiled as I spoke in my broken English. It seemed as if he liked how I looked and only gave me permission to enter and advised my brother to return home to his mother. It seemed that my brother's fragile and puny figure touched him with considerable sensitivity. He sincerely didn't want my brother to work at such a young age and so did not let him go through. Since I was healthier and presentable, I was quickly given permission to enter the base.

The corporal I was assigned to was a sympathetic young man, who also appeared to be in charge of the canteen. Immediately he gave me the job of cleaning up the canteen, to deliver products to soldiers who were encamped in tents that were numbered and easy to find. Hence on my first day I had made 10 piasters as my daily wages and on top of that another 10 piasters from tips. All in all, I had made 20 piasters in loose change. Working this way for two months, my mother had now a tidy sum.

As soon as we had accumulated a sufficient sum, I asked my mother to go to the nearby town of Ramle, a four-hour walk from our tent city. I definitely wanted to buy some clothing for her and my sisters, in spite of my mother's reluctance to spend the money and that we could use that saved up money for something more important. She always had the insecurity that we will be left penniless, like the Armenian proverb that says, "He who is bitten by a snake is afraid of the rope's shadow."

I stayed steadfast to my plan and demanded that we go that same day. Moreover the previous day I had asked permission from my captain to go buy clothing for my mother, which made the captain very happy. Finally that day we headed to Ramle, near Jaffa, and bought clothes for my mother and my two sisters, a coat for my brother, needles and some thread, and other various things like spoons and knives that were necessary in a household.

My joy was boundless. At last my mother and sisters were going to be free of their patchwork rags ... and I would be free to ask my mother to recall those prolonged agonizing and humiliating two years of separation. The next day, when I returned from work at the military base, my mom had already sewn dresses for herself and my sisters, as best as possible since she was not a seamstress. On returning home, in order to surprise me, the three of them greeted me adorned in their new dresses. My mother, considering me her support, hugged and kissed me with tears in her eyes. My sisters hugged and expressed their gratitude to their older brother. And I, also tearful and proud, asked for their old rags and instantly burned them, despite my mother's protests. Subsequently I was finally rid of that apparition that had pained me.

Chapter 8
MY MOTHER RECOUNTS

As I had mentioned earlier, we stayed in the Wadi es-Sarrar tent city for four months and then were transferred by train to the tent city of Port Said in Egypt, where the people of Suediya (Arabic for Mousa Dagh), had been relocated, following their successful, heroic self-defense battle. The British Army and the AGBU were in charge of Port Said tent city.[1] Before settling into the tents, they disinfected us along with our belongings. They gave us pieces of clothing and underwear. Also, they gave us mattresses made from grass and blankets. Carrying all these things, they took us to a tent where, for the first time since our ordeal began in 1915, my mother, brother, sisters, and I finally slept on beds, calmly and contentedly.

Tent City of Port Said, Suez Canal, 1915-1919

1 With the support of the AGBU Armenian General Benevolent Union, the British government established a tent city on the east bank of the Suez Canal, across from port said city to house 4,058 people who had fled after the heroic battle of Mousa Dagh. From September 13-15, these refugees moved to Egypt, with the people of Karadouran in Vadi es-Sarar settling nearby. The first doctor in the tent city was Serop Churikian from Kessab, and Rev. Fr. Bedros Paboujian of Karadouran conducted joint weddings for several couples.

The next morning we came out of the tent to view our surrounding. My mother, noticing that we all were well-dressed, had tears in her eyes since she recalled her first born, Hovsep, missing perhaps in Transjordan. "Dear God," she said, "please let my eldest son come here so that we are once again united as a family, and after that let Your will be done."

Newly arriving Kessab survivors would bring bits of news about my older brother. Some would say he was in Amman with the Circassians, others would say that the Circassians had murdered him during the retreat of the British. Until September 1918, we had no definitive news from him. Then all of a sudden we received a letter in my brother's handwriting. He was safe and sound in Jerusalem and would join us shortly. My mother dropped to her knees and showed her gratitude to God. We were overjoyed by this news.

After receiving the letter from my brother, I approached my mom and asked her to recount the story of their lives after I was taken to the orphanage. My mother was hesitant, perhaps because that episode of her life weighed heavily on her and she did not wish to recall those days of anguish. Upon my insistence, however, she gave in and started imparting the following story:

Mousa Dagh Armenians rescued by the French Navy

"My son, you definitely remember your father's passing away and our terrible financial situation during those days, particularly when the cursed epidemic that killed our family members. You would also know that a week after your father's death, I bore a pretty daughter. Barely 40 days after the birth, I had to go back to work in the forests to chop wood, which I carried on my back to sell in Salt. With the income from the wood I sold, I would bring home some wheat, flour, or some cash.

"Returning from Salt, I would prepare some soup for you. In my absence, your older brother, Hovsep, would look after the children. And this went on indefinitely. When Grandfather Mateos suggested taking you to the orphanage, despite the opposition that your uncles showed, I agreed as had you, thinking that if the epidemic would take all our lives, at least you would survive. With these dark thoughts and with a heavy heart I agreed to be separated from a piece of my heart and send you off to the orphanage. It is very tough for a mother to let go of her own flesh and blood, but in my opinion I deemed it the best choice.

"Abou Mussa el-Madi, the landlord, was a widower. He and his son, Musa, were rich Bedouin property owners and very decent people. Neither he nor his son ever looked into my eyes, despite me being a widow, 34 years old and pretty. He showed empathy and wished to help me out but did not wish me to think he was doing favors for free. So he would at times call me and tell me, 'Um-Yousef (Hovsep's mom), would you and Yousef hold this sack so I can fill it with wheat and take it to the mill?'

"And thus our job would be to hold the sack, so the landlord would fill the sacks with wheat from their clay silos, and his son, Musa, loading them on donkeys would take them to the mill. A while later his sister, Kazna, would bring us a sa'a (equivalent of 25 kilos) of wheat and tell us this was in return for our help. This same landlord during harvest season would set up tents on his fields, which were approximately two hours away. We asked him if he would let us glean. He not only obliged but allowed me and your brother to glean wheat and also pick the standing wheat stalks. Your brother had a pleasant voice so the reapers would ask him to sing, and your brother would sing Armenian songs he had learned from his father and glean at the same time. As compensation for his singing, in the presence and acknowledgment of our landlord, he would receive large quantities of wheat.

Tent city of Port Said, Egypt, 1915-1919

In the evenings I would bring the wheat home and grind the stalks on a stone to separate the husk from the seeds. In this way, I would prepare our winter supply. The first year, your brother and I for 10 days would set out early and return home at the end of the day. Our kind landlord, who was a 50-year-old Muslim Bedouin, suggested that he set up a tent for us on the field so that we stay there until the end of the reaping season.

Seeing my somber predicament he said, 'Why are you scared, my daughter? I will set up a tent beside mine, and rest assured that nothing will happen to you. You need to understand, Um-Yousef, that the Bedouins are always helpful, without disrespecting your honor.'

"I accepted his offer and asked him to rent, on my behalf, two donkeys so I could bring my children and things.

"The old man said, 'What a shame! As long as I am here, you ask another person's pack animal? My son, Musa, tomorrow go to Um-Yousef's home with two of our donkeys and bring her children and things here.'

"And so it was done. During the reaping season we stayed in the field. Near his own tent, he set up a small tent made of goat hair rugs, confirming that our things will be safe and the other Bedouins will not dare steal. For weeks we gleaned, and we filled two sacks with wheat.

"During those times there was a shortage of food, and I developed an eye disease, night blindness, and I was not able to see at night. As a result I had to feed my family before sunset, because I couldn't see after dark. Your one-year-old newborn sister, who was very thin because of malnutrition, suddenly fell ill while we were staying on the field. Realizing that she might die, I wanted to go to the village, to Fuhais, so she could die at home and that I could bury your sister next to her father. I told your brother, Hovsep, to go home to ask Uncle Zenop to give him the only donkey left from late Grandfather George so I could take the child home.

"Uncle Zenop allegedly had said, 'Janym (my dear one, Turkish), why bring her home? If she is going to die, bury her in the field, and that'll be it.'

"Deprivation and misery have taken their toll on the people to a point that the same uncle who cared for everyone in the family so much now had become stone-hearted and very simply, without any ill-intent toward me, refused to hand over the donkey. When your brother returned and told me what happened, I started to wail and weep.

"At that instance Abou Mussa el-Madi quietly came to us and inquired the reason for my weeping. I was so mournful and because my Arabic was weak, I was unable to say anything. But your brother, Hovsep, who knew enough Arabic, explained in detail to Abou Mussa el-Madi what had happened.

"Abou Mussa, saddened, got angry, asking, 'Why did you send the boy? We have donkeys in the field.'

"I told the landlord that I didn't want to abuse his kindness. That is why I sent Hovsep to Uncle Zenop for the donkey, and my brother-in-law had refused.

"The Bedouin landlord ordered his son, Musa, by saying, 'Come immediately, my son, and load Um-Yousef's wheat sacks and other belongings on the donkey and take them home in Fuhais.'

"Truly that same evening he got us home where, a day later, your newborn sister passed away, and we buried her next to your father, Minas. I didn't have the desire to go back to the field after this sad event, especially when I had already saved sufficient staples at home.

"One day a Bedouin friend of the landlord asked me if I would give him

10-year-old Nishan to be his cowherd. He had realized that we were needy and that there would be one less mouth to feed. So, I gave him Nishan to be his cowherd. Hovsep went to Amman to try his luck. Later I heard that he had become a shepherd for a Circassian. Your sisters and I were the ones who were left at home. I was hardly able to look after them in my weak state of health. Still, I would sometimes go to the forest to get wood to sell in Salt. And so life continued this way. By the spring of 1917, my brother, your Uncle Avedis, came from Salt, fearing that we would be infected with typhus fever, and took us to his home in Al- Salt. Then I think he left for Amman (probably to look for work). Nishan, being bored with cow herding, came home to Salt.

"In the meantime, I became infected with typhus in my brother's home and became bedridden. A few days later I began to rave with no one to take care of me and all alone except for my children, your 10 or 11-year-old brother, Nishan, and 8 or 9-year-old your sister, Sara. My condition was so bad that I was unable to think and couldn't understand what was happening around me.

The kids would buy some milk with whatever change they found and would take care of me. Your sister and brother, who would go without food, had no other choice but to beg for money in the streets, which was a heart-wrenching time in the lives of my children, but they were desperate and had to go to that measure.

"Luckily I did not die of the typhus epidemic and gradually began to recover my health back, but I was so weak, and regretfully I was forced to permit and even advise my little ones to find a piece of bread, to beg, for all our sakes. This situation continued for a month.

"My kids would tell me, crying, 'Mum, sometimes they would shoo us away, and other times they would give us only a portion of a loaf of bread.'

"Not all portions of bread were the same size. One day, the wretched ones, having only been gone for an hour, returned home with many pieces and with a few coins. This time, the portion sizes were uniform. Upon my insistence, they explained that a kind man had given them a big loaf of bread and a few coins so they decided not to stay outside longer. To deceive their mother, they sliced the bread into equal portions to show that they had gotten the bread from different people. I was so touched with what had happened, I found what they did was right and cried long and hard....

"Fortunately my brother returned from Amman. Even though he had no work, which I knew, he would go to the vegetable gardens and, out of desperation, would steal what he could find so that he could feed his sister and his orphaned nieces. This continued for months when one day, fearing he would be caught, my brother fled to Jerusalem. By then I had regained my strength and started to offer my services to the Arab neighbors so I could get a piece of bread for my little ones.

"More or less, this was the way we were able to survive the winter of 1917, when the British Army entered Al-Salt without opposition. A week later we noticed that yet again they retreated, and the exiled Armenians fled to Jerusalem as the British Army retreated toward Jerusalem. I, too, although weak like your brother and sisters and concerned about your older brother, was forced to take the children and leave. Since no pack animals were in sight and neither having the finances to either buy one or rent one, I was unable to take a lot of things with me. Therefore, I put the copper vessel on Sarah's head, and I carried some plates, towels, one blanket, and Zabel, your sister, on one of my shoulders. Nishan, feeling unwell then, caught my skirt, and we walked toward Jericho.

"When we got to Ghor, in the Jordan valley, the German planes started bombing roads. Often, in order to protect ourselves, we would throw ourselves in the bushes or lay down on the ground for shelter. When we approached the Jordan River, the driver of a British Army truck, who took pity on my children and my pitiful appearance, gave us a lift in his lorry until Jericho. From Jericho to Jerusalem, spending the nights under the stars, we barely made it to shelter in the David Castle military barracks near the St. James Monastery. You found us there that day, when you came all by yourself from the orphanage to see us.

"And so my child, in your absence, this was our darabalits (painful) life in exile. I have a favor to ask you, my son. If by chance you stay alive, I want you to one day go, no matter how long has passed, to the village of Mehes, where your father had passed away, and visit his grave and pray. Do your utmost to visit that kind landlord, his son, and grandchildren and, on my behalf, thank that unschooled but kind and noble Bedouin as I will never forget that man's compassion.

"After your father passed away, I am certain that all of you would have died of starvation if he had not extended a helping hand during our burdensome times. I am telling this to all of you, and whoever of you is able to, should one of those days visit the family and show our gratefulness and thankfulness. And if you are capable of doing so, when you visit them, remember to take presents to that generous and dignified Bedouin."

And with this, with tearful eyes, my mother concluded her sad story. Clearly my mother narrated the part of her life I did not know. The rest I will portray. I must note that to this day, my mother, who is now 75, when she comes across a beggar, recalling how her children were once beggars, will always hand out either some money, food, or clothing.

Chapter 9
PORT SAID

After settling down in the Port Said camp I immediately started thinking of school and employment. I applied to the Sisuan Primary School[1] Administration and was admitted to the third grade of the elementary section. My younger brother was admitted to kindergarten. We would be at school 'til noon and, in the afternoon as I was free, I spoke to the chief security officer of the camps and suggested to him that my services were available and that I was willing to work in the kitchen, perhaps as a cook's helper.

Unlike the other exiles, I knew some English words, which were appreciated by the British soldiers. They accepted me to work for four Egyptian pounds per month. At noon I would work in the dining room area, and later in the afternoon I would carry out orders from soldiers, like getting them cigarettes, bringing them soda, cleaning and polishing their shoes. I would earn extra income besides my monthly salary. This went on 'til the spring of 1919, earning enough that my mother, brother, and sisters got new clothes and shoes. They were not in need of anything. My mother also started working in the kitchens of the camp for a minimal salary.

My older brother, Hovsep, returned from Jerusalem at the end of 1918. My mother's joy and our delight were boundless. After the British Army had retreated, the Circassians, for whom my poor brother was a shepherd, had threatened to throw him into a well. But thank God, they hadn't carried out their threat. So he fled to Jerusalem, walking all the way. From there in a caravan, and at the British expense, he joined us in the Port Said camp.

Outside of work and school, I signed up as a Sisuan School scout. I think I was the youngest among the scouts. The leader of the scouts was an Englishman, Mr. Reynold, who later became the principal of the Saint George College of Jerusalem for many years. There five to six students from Mousa Dagh studied at his expense.

1 Named after Sis, the capital of the Armenian Kingdom of Cilicia (Sisuan in Arabic; Kozan in Turkish), the Sisuan School was opened by the AGBU in the Port Said refugee camp. The school accommodated 1,253-2,225 students in both boys' and girls' sections, including a kindergarten and elementary school. It closed in 1919.

Since the Suez Canal[2] waterway was nearby, I spent all my free time with my friends in the water. I had become an expert swimmer and diver. After passing the exams, I became a lifeguard for swimmers and divers and received, as a sign of appreciation, scout medals. During holidays we would spend almost all our time in the waters of the canal. Occasionally, four or five of us would swim to the opposite (west) bank of the canal, where a freshwater stream flows in the Suez Canal salt water and where we fished or stole fish from nets strung by the park rangers.

Hovsep, Kevork's older brother

It was pleasant to see peers like ourselves, stuffing our hats with pyjamas, bread, and a match with our hat laces tied under our chin, crossing the canal to the other (west) bank. There we would put on our pajamas and would begin our most pleasant and risky adventures, the best of which was stealing fish from the nets. Two of us would stand

2 The Suez Canal is an artificial sea-level waterway in Egypt, connecting the Mediterranean Sea to the Red Sea. Built by the Suez Canal Company between 1859 and 1869.

guard, looking for park rangers while the other two would jump into the freshwater stream and lift the fishnet that the park rangers had spread from one side of the canal to the other — the freshwater stream was only three to four meters wide. We would skewer 5-10 fishes through a branch. Then we would swim through the saltwater canal dragging the skewered fish behind us. We would get to the other side of the canal and walk back to the camp.

Port Said city located west of the Suez Canal.

There were times during our risk-taking adventures when a park ranger chased after us but, to avoid being caught, we would jump into the canal and swim back toward the east bank. If he had started throwing stones at us, we would have swum far off or we would have dived underwater below the surface so the stones would not harm our bodies.

On November 11, 1918, on the day of the ceasefire,[3] a military parade was going to take place in Port Said. The Sisuan School Scout Marching

3 World War I ended on November 11, 1918, some 11 days after the Armistice of Mudros was signed on October 30, 1918.The Ottoman government had no other choice but to sign the agreement since their armies were crushed and the allies had made it clear that they would continue invading if a treaty of surrender was not signed.

Band and scouts with their marching melodies participated in the fanfare, which lasted several hours. During the afternoon the members of the National Union[4] served us lunch in a restaurant. Until this day, I remember a certain Miss Rosa Kalfaian, who embraced me for being the youngest scout, sat at a table, and served me lovingly.

Kevork Manjikian with Mr. Reynolds, the leader of the Boy Scouts

In the spring of 1919, camp authorities started sending the exiled survivors back to their native soil. Hovsep, my brother, had a wish to return to Kessab as fast as possible so he could prepare the house for our return home, but his requests were denied. I got news that a small ship with some residents of Kessab would be leaving for Latakia, which

4 After 1915, Egyptian-Armenians founded the Armenian National Union (ANU). Its major purpose was to locate and identify survivors of the Armenian genocide and return them to their appropriate places. In 1918, with the war still on the outskirts of Damascus, the ANU, with no further delay, gathered Armenian refugee women and children who were left behind with Arab families. National Union outposts were established in places like Damascus, Aleppo, Adana, and Kessab.

is near Kessab, at the expense of the state. Yet again, they did not allow my brother to get on that ship.

Hovsep and wife Kalila Yaralian. Kalila lived to live until age 104.

I decided to insert my brother as a stowaway on that ship's passenger list. Since I was serving the chief of military security personnel, I was permitted to use their small boat, which I rowed splendidly. So that day I asked for permission to use the boat for rowing exercise. Naturally I hid Hovsep, my brother, in the boat with his mattress and belongings. I rowed from the camp for about 500 meters to the harbor.

The ship that was going to transport exiles had a waist-high deck railing. I rowed to the opposite side of the boarding rail, tied my boat to the railing, jumped on the deck, and engaged the guard in small talk. He was a member of the brigade controlled by the chief security guard, from whom I had received permission to use the boat. I had instructed my brother that as soon as I engaged the guard, he should throw his belongings on board the ship and, once he himself jumped on board, disappear in the crowd of exiles.

As we had agreed, while I was talking to the guard, who was standing on the boarding ladder, my brother, who was on the other side, after throwing his belongings on deck, jumped on board himself, and mingled with the Kessab passengers. When I noticed in my peripheral vision that my brother was safely on the ship, I left the guard, who was impressed at how I, a tiny 13-year-old, was able to row a distance of 500 meters.

He walked with me to the starboard side to see how I rowed my way back. I got on the boat that was tied to the ship, said goodbye, and headed back. After the passenger ship departed, I told the same guard what had really happened. After this guard heard what had really happened, he was so amused he told the story to his colleagues. They labeled me "a contraband smuggler." I didn't care. What mattered was that my brother had left the camp so he could put his ancestral house in order and make it livable prior to our return.

Chapter 10
HOMEWARD BOUND

In August of 1919, our family decided to leave for Aleppo by train along with a caravan made up of 350 Cilicians. Then everyone would disperse to their places of origin.[1] Those types of caravans used to have a single passport with a single passenger list (350 people), which included the name of the caravan leader — I think he was from the city of Sis — and the name of the interpreter, who was me. Even though I was merely 13 years old, I was the only one who knew some English. The passport also had the total number of the exiles — how many were men and how many were women and children. This passport and passenger list were used for the purpose of food distribution. At each station we stopped, the military authorities would supply a day's worth of food to the exiles based on the information on that passport. The food supply would be handed over to the caravan leader and interpreter, who were then supposed to distribute it to the exiled ones.

So at designated stations one of the local military men would call out, looking for the caravan leader and the interpreter. As soon as they saw me, a young teenager, laughter would break out. Sometimes a giant of a soldier as a joke would place me on his shoulder, taking me to his superior, and introducing me to him by saying, "And this is who they call their interpreter."

Despite this comedic scene, they would give us all the necessary food supply, which was transported to the wagons by some of the exiles. At the wagons, according to the list, each would get his share. Let me also mention that we used to travel in freight cars. On those journeys our food supply consisted of bread, biscuits, canned meat, and cheese.

1 The exiled Kessab residents who survived the retreat of the Turkish troops began to return to their villages. "The survivors from Kessab returned in groups," Movsess Shahbazian said and described the condition of the first arrivals. "The scene was moving. The once flourished village had become ruins and the streets unrecognizable. The gardens and orchards were wastelands. Kessab has become a habitat for wildlife. And the people returning from deportation were in a miserable situation. Utterly depressed, hungry and weak. They had barely escaped the clutches of death. Those who lacked direct livelihoods lived, for months, on wild fruits, grass, and by doing odd jobs here and there." (Shahbazian, Movsess (1965). The Armenian Volunteer Movement in World War 1, 1917-1920. (pp.28-29). Kessab, Syria.)

Within a week we traveled by rail to Haifa from Port Said. In Haifa, they settled us in a camp, where we stayed for an additional month. Again we headed to Aleppo by rail.

Garabet, Kevork's uncle, 1920s

When we got to Aleppo, we ran across Uncle Garabet at the station. During the deportation, he walked with the caravan until our first stop past the city of Ordou. He then fled back to Kessab and later stayed in the Jisr al-Shughur region for the entire duration of the deportations. Our joy was boundless for this accidental reunion. Hearing that an immigrant caravan was coming from Port Said, my uncle came to the station to get some news of his relatives when he suddenly saw us. What happiness for him and for us!

Our uncle was alive — and the youngest and most favored of my father and mother. When they took us to the Aleppo *kaghtagayan* (refugee exile center), my uncle came with us. He helped us and told us that after ditching us during the first night of exile at Jisr al-Shughur, he had returned to the Kessab region with other friends. There they hid in the forests of our village. Gradually the Turkish gendarmes emptied Kessab and its region. Nearby Turkish villagers looted its properties and set some houses on fire. My uncle and his friends witnessed all these. Since it was not possible to stay in those deserted areas any longer, my uncle went from Kessab to Jisr al-Shughur. He served an Arab landowner and remained there throughout the duration of the war without any news from his relatives. When Syria was occupied by the Allies (Turkey and Germany had surrendered and ceasefire prevailed), Uncle Garabet went to Aleppo, where he worked for the American Near East Relief.[2] As a student at the Aintab College, he had been studying English when the war broke out.

French General Gouraud entering Aleppo, September 13, 1920

During the few days of our stay in Aleppo, my mother decided to return to Kessab with my sisters and convinced my brother and me

2 American humanitarians who had helped the Armenian refugees in 1915 established the Near East American Auxiliary Committee in 1918. On August 6, 1919, renamed the American Near East Relief, it helped Armenian refugee-sponsored schools and orphanages and donated large funds to more than 50 centers, including in Aleppo, Beirut, Damascus and Soviet Armenian until 1929.

to remain in Aleppo at Aharon's (Reverend Shirajian's) orphanage.[3] My uncle informed us that although my brother Hovsep was back in Karadouran, our home was unlivable, and we had to live in another house temporarily. "For that reason," my uncle said, "until we are in a position to move into our homes, it would be best for Nishan and you live in the orphanage for a few years."

Having found our uncle's proposal pragmatic, my mother placed Nishan and me in the orphanage with his help, and then my uncle sent my sisters and mother to Kessab via Antioch.[4] Nearly every Sunday while we were in the orphanage, we visited our Uncle Garabet, who would give us pocket money that satisfied our boyish needs.

Kevork and Nishan at Aharonian Orphanage, Aleppo, Syria 1919.

3 Pastor Aharon Shirajian was the founder and first director of the Armenian orphanage-school (1915-1924). Dr. Asadour Altunian, the owner of a hospital that cared for the Ottoman Army during WWI, played a big role in the survival and development of this orphanage. (For further reference, read Khatchig Mouradian's 2021 book, *The Resistance Network: The Armenian Genocide and Humanitarianism in Ottoman Syria 1915-1918)*.

4 *Antakya* in Arabic, Antioch today is the capital of Hatay Province (Sanjak of Alexandretta to Syrians), the southernmost province of Turkey. While the province came under French mandate after WWI, the French agreed to incorporate it back into the Republic of Turkey in 1939. This caused the immigration of the Armenian communities of Mousa Dagh to Syria and mostly to the Lebanese village of Anjar in the Bekaa Valley, where the French had already arranged their settlement and built one-room houses for each family. Anjar still exists today. Syria still claims the Sanjak of Alexandretta as its own until today.

Sometimes I would give a *barghut* (very low value Ottoman coin) to Nishan, who appeared to be a very well-behaved boy, so he would go and buy us pomegranates or roasted chickpeas or some sweets. On many occasions, he would buy several things with a single barghut. And sometimes with his purchases, he would return to the orphanage with the money in hand. When I asked him how it was that he could buy so many things with only one barghut, he would answer that the shopkeepers wouldn't take money from him, etc.

This situation repeated itself a couple of times. Once I realized of what was going on, I decided to follow him to see how he was shopping with one barghut. He went to a store that sold halva with the barghut in his hand. Once the grocer had weighed the halva and placed it on the table, he got busy with other customers. Taking advantage of this opportunity, Nishan very slowly lifted the halva and walked away unnoticed, without paying. Further on he stopped at a fruit stall and selected four or five pomegranates. Once again at the moment that the grocer was distracted by other customers, he took the pomegranates and walked away. I realized then that he was getting used to stealing.

When he returned to the orphanage school and wanted to convince me with his lies, as if the shopkeepers wouldn't take money, I kicked him hard. I warned him to stop and that if he did this one more time, I would hand him over to the shopkeepers. From then on, he stopped this habit.

In the Aharon orphanage, approximately 2,000 rescued orphans found refuge. Five to six hundred of them were girls. The orphanage had three buildings: two accommodated the boys and the other, the girls. With such a huge multitude, it was very difficult to properly feed and clothe them right after the war. For example, in the morning each was given one dry loaf of bread and for all six of us one communal copper bowl of tea, which we were obliged to drink without a cup. Therefore, we were obliged to gulp down tea with teaspoons first in a hurry without softening the dry bread in tea. If we attempted to combine the tea with dry bread, the other friends would quickly gulp down the tea and would leave only three or four spoons of tea for the others. It should be said that the noon and evening meals, although not so tasty, were enough to satisfy us.

Bread was plentiful, but the cleanliness was weak. The management put my brother in the kindergarten of the orphanage and enrolled me in the elementary fifth grade of the Haigazian School.[5] A few months later, Uncle Garabet came to the orphanage and gave us a couple of *mejid*[6] for pocket money. Then he left for Kessab. Four or five months after my uncle's departure, my brother and I got infected with leprosy that was going around in the orphanage. So once a week, they would take us to the Arabic baths for a hard scrub. They would wash us and then disinfect us with some type of medicine mixed with sulphur.

Having somewhat recovered this way, I thought of escaping from the orphanage with my brother and somehow getting to Kessab. In order to do that, we needed sufficient funds. We only had two or three mejid, and in those times, as a result of the Kemalist movement, all roads to Kessab were closed by the Kemalists. When my Uncle Garabet was in Aleppo, he gave me the address of Dikran, who was my father's first cousin in America.

Through my uncle I was acquainted with the workers of the Near East Relief and with the chauffeurs, who would sometimes drive up to Iskenderoun (Alexandretta). So I wrote a letter to our relative in America, Dikran Manjikian, and explained to him who we were because he had never met us. He knew my father. I told him that presently we were in the orphanage and would like to go to Kessab and join our mother, but we had no money. I asked him to send us travel money. A couple of months later in January of 1920, I got a reply from him. In the envelope was a check. When cashed, it amounted to five Ottoman pounds and a few mejid. Without wasting any time, I went to the Near East offices, where I met with one of their drivers, who I knew was one of my uncle's friends. I asked him to help us find a way to drive to Iskenderun.[7] Beyond Antioch, we would find a way to get to Kessab. Although the man tried to convince us to remain in the orphanage, seeing that we were determined to run away, he gave in. He would take us with him, two days later when it was his turn to drive to Kerek-Khan (near Iskenderun). He ordered us to wait for him in front of the office around 5 a.m. that day.

5 The teachers of the Kharpert American College played a big role in its 1919 founding.

6 *Mejid* or *mejide*: 1 Ottoman pound = 5 Mejidie = 100 ghuroosh, 1 Mejidie = 20 ghuroosh, 1 ghuroosh = 40 para

7 Iskenderun, Alexandretta, originally a swampy and deserted place, in the mid-nineteenth century turned into a developing seaport, where a large number of Armenians from Beylan, Suediya, and Kessab among other places, went to settle. The Apostolic and Evangelical churches existed in the city before 1915. Before the deportation, there used to be a large community of people from Kessab in Iskenderun that kept ties with Kessab. These people financially assisted the Armenian Apostolic Church and school in Kessab.

That same evening, we started getting ready. On the designated day, we put our worn-out clothes in blankets. Tying them at the ends, we gave them the look of bags. At 4:30 in the morning, carrying the bags, we quietly left the orphanage and headed to the Near East Relief office. Sometime later, the driver came in the huge truck loaded with merchandise and sat us on the merchandise, covered with a thick canvas. It was a cold winter morning. Two brothers, leaning on the cotton bales, covering themselves with the blankets in order not to catch a cold. At around 4 p.m. in the afternoon, we arrived at Kerek-Khan. Before heading to Antioch, he handed us over to an Armenian innkeeper, ordering him to find us shelter for the night and somehow to put us on a coach to Iskenderun the next morning.

You can imagine our audacity. I was only14 years old, my brother was only 11, and we were going to Iskenderun, an unfamiliar city, where we knew no one. From there we had to plan our seaside journey to Kessab all by ourselves, but our adolescent imagination had taken flight. We wanted to see our mother as soon as possible.

"There will be a way. *Asdvats voghormats e* (God is merciful) ..." I kept reminding myself.

The next morning the Armenian inn keeper put us on our way to Iskenderun. He rented a horse-drawn cart that was transporting goods. In return for our passage, we agreed to pay him three mejid. Because of the bumpy road, the cart shook, but it helped our digestion. As soon as we got to Iskenderun, we went to the first restaurant we saw and in Arabic asked them to bring us food.

They delayed in serving us immediately. Our orphan clothes made them suspicious, and they had second thoughts for bringing us food. Perhaps they feared that we were poor and couldn't pay for the food. Angry, I told them in Arabic, "Here is the money," and showed it to them. And I added to hurry up and bring us food. I started mumbling in Armenian, "What kind of useless people they are. They won't even feed us because we look like poor beggars...."

Hearing this the owner of the restaurant immediately approached us and asked us in Armenian, "Who are you, and where are you from?" When he learned we were from Kessab and were from the Manjikian family, he switched to the Kessab dialect because he was from Kessab as well. He said that my senior Uncle Zenop's son, Serop, and the husband of my Aunt Zarouhi (married to Elias Seferian) were staying in Iskenderun, and they would come to this restaurant for dinner every evening. After we finished eating and walked around the city for a while, we returned to the restaurant to wait for my cousin. At 7 in the evening, they came. Their surprise was big when suddenly they saw us. Although they were happy, hearing our intention for travel, they were concerned and said that all roads to Kessab by way of Antioch, full of Kemalist *chetehs* (bandits), were absolutely closed off.

My cousin and my aunt's husband with other workers from Kessab, 8-10 people, mostly workers as *stevedores* (dock workers), had rented a large hall. They gave us a corner in that hall, where we slept on the floor. Covered with our only blanket, we went to sleep. Naturally our relatives didn't have a spare mattress to give us, and those of the workers weren't better than ours.

Realizing that there was no route through Antioch, we decided to temporarily study at the local Armenian national school. Having stayed in Iskenderun for a whole month, I started musing over the idea of going to Latakia by sea and from there find a way to get to Kessab. Our cousin got tired of hearing repetitions of our wish to find a way to reach Kessab, so he booked us on one of the ships belonging to the Italian Sitmar Lines Company that would take us from Iskenderun to Latakia. And so this way we left for Latakia.

Since Latakia was unfamiliar to us, we started looking for an Armenian in the harbor. Luckily we met a compatriot and asked him to show us the American hospital and Dr. Balf. Since childhood, I had heard that this American missionary doctor had sponsored my father's education in Latakia and may have treated him. Encouraged by the information, I tried to find this kind man to ask him for a temporary shelter for my brother and me until I could find a way to go to Kessab. If that would not transpire, then we would stay in an inn because we still had five Ottoman pounds in our pockets.

Thus with cautious steps we approached the oversized metal gates of the hospital and rang the bell. One of the servants, thinking that we were beggars, came out and attempted to drive us away. When I explained that we were from the Manjikian family and that Dr. Balf knew our father Minas, I insisted that we see Dr. Balf. The door keeper, who must have been working in the hospital for many years, remembered my father and allowed his orphans inside. Almost half an hour later, the aged American Missionary physician came and welcomed us.

Half in Armenian and half in English, we made him understand that we were the orphans of Minas Manjikian, for whose schooling he had helped. Recalling at once, he took us in and arranged for us to have a good bath. His staff gave us new underwear that — I don't know how — fit us perfectly. He said that if needed, he could put us up in the hospital area for a few months until we found the occasion to continue to Kessab.

In the evening after a splendid dinner, we went to a separate bedroom with two grand beds. Laying on the soft mattresses and covers, we went to sleep. All during the exile period we hadn't slept in such beautiful and comfortable beds. At night I suddenly woke up because of the softness of the bed, and I couldn't believe it. It was like I was in a dream from *A Thousand and One Nights* because orphans like us, who had been under years of anguish and torture, never expected such human kindness and care.

In the morning, we woke up and washed in front of clean sinks. They gave us separate breakfasts, serving each of us individually, and at noon they gave us lunch. This went on for two weeks.

During that time, we would systematically visit every inn we could, looking for a way to reach Kessab. On our third day of our search, we came across 8-10 young men from Kessab in a *khan* (inn). In that group, by chance, we saw our relative, nicknamed Ketche Hourkourar (who had married my father's uncle's daughter). When he heard our intention to travel immediately to Kessab, he said that for now that was impossible.

However, the next day we overheard that Ketche's group and another group, a total of 20 armed men, planned to leave with a 12-mule caravan[8] loaded with food supplies. Ketche Hourkourar was also in that group. As soon as I heard this, I quickly ran to Ketche, pleading with him to take us with him, but he categorically refused. "I can't take on such a big responsibility, Kevork," he said. "Since we are leaving as an armed force, most probably we will encounter the chetehs (Turkish Kemalist irregular forces) on the way. There may be fighting, casualties, and death. We aren't even sure if we will arrive in one piece."

8 Before the appearance of cars, donkeys and mules were the main source of transportation in mountainous areas like Kessab. Coaches were almost never used. Imports and exports to and from the Kessab market were done by mule drivers, who were renowned for their bravery and their fluency in the Turkish and Arabic languages.

All our pleas and our offers to give cash for their services or renting a mule, etc. were in vain. He unconditionally ignored all our offers. Even his friends refused our plan. They advised us to stay for a few months with Dr. Balf until the roads were safe again.

Absolutely hopeless I walked away from them. Luckily using my wit with the khan owner, I found out their day of departure. They had decided to set out two days later at 4 in the morning. Without saying anything to anyone I informed Doctor Balf that we were leaving early next morning and asked him to let the guard wake us up at 3 a.m. in the morning. Dr. Balf gave instructions to have food prepared for our road trip, and the security guard woke us up at 3 a.m. precisely. As we collected our belongings, I eyed the two covers we had been using for two weeks at Dr. Balf's, and I wanted to exchange them with the ones we had.

Nishan reminded me, "That would be considered theft. Didn't you beat me up at the orphanage for stealing?"

I realized I was wrong, so we took our own blankets instead and tied the ends to give them the appearance of bags and carrying them left our warm rooms and headed toward the khan.

Nishan, Kevork's younger brother, Paris 1931

On that cold late January day with cloudless skies and a full moon, we sat next to a wall 20 meters away from the khan. From a distance we saw that they were loading the mules in a hurry. Around 4 a.m., these armed young men, masking their weapons under their cloaks, started hurriedly on their way with the pack animals before them. They headed toward the Latakia-Kessab Road. When their caravan was 300 to 400 meters away, we came out of our hiding place and quickly started to follow the caravan, always keeping a distance of 200 to 300 meters. We walked this way for two to three hours before we caught up with the caravan as it reached a place called Guendel,[9] a gorge with plenty of water.

Then began the uphill climb through the forests toward Kessab. When they saw us, could not believe their eyes and started forcing us to turn back using threats. But it did not work. We started crying, asking them to let us walk alongside them and that we didn't need to sit on mules. Finally seeing that we had covered a lot of distance, it wasn't proper to leave two young boys behind in the wilderness unprotected. They had no choice but to take us with them. Whatever awaited them would await us as well. My brother and I were ecstatic. We started munching on a fruit called *hembalas* (blueberry-like fruit) that grew on the roadside and happily were trying to keep up with their pace.

When we started the uphill climb in the forest, we felt tired. They were forced to place us on the mules and even handed us their Martin rifles, which we hung on our shoulders with pride. In those days, because of the Turkish irregulars, you couldn't even find a bird in the forests.

Because the caravan was carrying desperately needed ammunition and food supplies to Kessab, four of the armed boys guarded it from the right hillside of the road and another four from the left side hills of the road. Fortunately, with extreme caution, we arrived safely at Kessab around 9 p.m. The people were greatly excited to see the caravan, and even some of them greeted us at the entrance of Douzaghaj (the first roadside village before entering the Kessab township).

When we arrived at the center of Kessab Township, my brother and I with our belongings headed to my Aunt Zarouhi's house. Her husband,

9 Ghundeel Turkish, or Wadi Qandeel in Arabic, is a valley dotted by Alawite villages. The Alawites are a distinct sect of Islam.Turkmen villages are further north along the road and mountains.

as mentioned above, was in Iskenderun. When we reached their house and entered, we saw that our cousins, Krikor, 11, and Nishan, 9, were sitting around the hearth to get warm. When they saw us, they probably thought we were some orphan boys[10] from Kessab. They invited us in to get warm and offered us some bread and cheese.

"Where is your mother?" I asked. "We want to see her."

"There's no need to see her. We will give you whatever you need." With a kind and childlike simplicity, they wanted to be helpful to orphans, offering according to their traditional rural hospitality. When we told them we were their cousins, both of them ran to the balcony and started shouting, "Come Mother, our cousins, George and Nishan, have fallen from heaven...."

My aunt thought that her children were yelling because they were in danger, so she raced over from the neighbor's house. And what did she see? She saw her brother's two orphaned children...grown up. My beloved paternal Aunt Zarouhi was the only aunt, one of three sisters, who had survived the genocide. Before she had married, she had loved and raised me as a child. Seeing us, my aunt looked speechless for a few seconds because she was surprised and full of joy. Hugging us, she kissed us nonstop. And later came the flood of questions: "How are you? Where are you coming from? What a surprise. Not even a bird can return to Kessab, and how did you get here?"

My aunt immediately set the table. After supper, we wanted to go to bed. We let my aunt know that we still had symptoms of leprosy and that it would be a good idea for her to wash all our shirts and underwear well the next day. After having a nice bath, we slept and forgot all our fatigue until the next morning.

10 After the Mudros ceasefire, when Turkey surrendered to the Allies, Kessab had two orphanages: one in the Latin Cathedral, led by Father Sabatino Del Gaizo, and another in the central square's Evangelical building, overseen by Dayi (Ovsia Saghdjian) under the National Union. Each housed several hundred orphans, both boys and girls.

Chapter 11
KARADOURAN

In the morning, my aunt dropped everything she was doing and took us to our village, Karadouran[1], to our mother. My mother, my brother Hovsep, and my sisters' surprise and happiness were boundless. It was the first time after the 1915 Genocide that I had set foot in my birthplace. Everything seemed charming and beautiful to me, and all the scenery and the neighborhood resembled a scene from a movie. I recalled my childhood days, and in front of our ancestral home my mind wandered back to those happy and peaceful days when my grandfather and grandmother had been still alive. I remembered all those losses that we had in Arabia. Today our emptied village looked sad without them.

Our house was demolished. Our family had been living temporarily with the Kazazians. And we would for months go to the nearby stream to wash and to cover our bodies with sulfur until we were cured of the leprosy that infected us in the orphanage. In 1920, my Uncle Garabet was the local school's teacher, and we immediately enrolled to school there.

A month after we arrived, the Kessab Fedayeen Youth (a self-defense force), led by the Dayi of Kessab, Ovsia Saghdjian,[2] looted and burned a selected number of the neighboring Turkish villages, whose inhabitants both in the 1909 Adana massacres and in the 1915 Genocide had looted and burned our villages.[3] Nishan and I joined in the burning of Ordou.

1 Currently called Al-Samra in Syrian Arab Republic.

2 The legionnaires returned to Kessab after the French Army entered Cilicia. The first to leave the Legion would be Ovsia Saghdjian (Kara Oghlan or Dayi) and Missak Guiragosian (Missako or Sakhallie). "The services of these brave young men remain unforgettable in the heroic battle of Kessab self-defense," Movsess Shahbazian told of their odyssey. "When the world was not yet peaceful, the brave boys mentioned above decided with exceptional audacity to set out for Kessab. They left Mersin in military uniforms and weapons and passed through many Turkoman villages. They reached Kessab in two weeks. First, they thought of not revealing themselves to the locals. So they took refuge on the western slope of Kessab, in the seaside village of Karadouran. They had terrified people everywhere.... After some time, they came to Kessab township and introduced themselves to the locals!" (Shahbazian, p. 31.)

3 In 1919, two additional groups, having left the Armenian Foreign Legion in a similar manner, arrived in the Kessab region. Inspired by the volunteer movement, the local population began to venture freely and boldly into nearby Turkish villages, demanding the return of goods and livestock that rightfully belonged to them. Terrified of the Sakhallie (the bearded men), the Turkish villagers willingly repaid their debts and returned what they had unlawfully taken from the people of Kessab. However, by the spring of 1919, the southern and eastern borders of Kessab became increasingly dangerous. On several occasions,

One morning we heard that the village of Ordou had been surrounded by our defense forces, and the people of Kessab were rushing there behind the fighters. Learning of this, Nishan and I, without telling my mother, went to Kessab, which is a one-hour walking distance from our village. From there we arrived in Ordou around noon. We heard gunfire from Ordou's surroundings but noticing the traffic of our people, we too entered the village.

Karadouran, Al Samra in Arabic, Syrian Arab Republic

The village was totally abandoned; not a single soul except the Kessabtsis defense forces were wandering around the village to protect the people from any Turkish counterattacks. We witnessed that some houses were already on fire, so Nishan and I lit firewood and went into houses where we piled up clothing or wooden things and burned them. Together we burned four houses this way.

We never thought of robbing but only of taking revenge. We thought that by trashing the houses of Turks, we would avenge ourselves from

volunteers engaged in battles with Turkmen villagers, looting and destroying their settlements. The spoils were subsequently distributed among the survivors.. (Tcholakian [1995], pp. 111-112.)

those destructive Turks, many of whom robbed and destroyed our forefathers' houses. Even if we had wished to loot the houses, we were not strong enough to carry the items very far. However, we wanted some memorabilia from that Turkish village. In a house I found a new mattress and a blanket, and Nishan found a beautiful sickle, which we used for a long time as a souvenir. But the people, either on their backs or on pack animals, carried away what they could. However, at the border of the Kessab Township, a then-temporary Armenian government collected 10 percent tax from each person as part of the fighters' share.

Ovsia Saghdejian, Kessab's "Dayi," circa 1950

It needs to be mentioned that the then Kessab "government"[4] was really a Fedayeen self-defense force of the Kessabtsis. They also had a National

4 Kevork's quotation marks highlight two key government entities in the lives of the Armenians of Kessab. The first, the National Union, was formed in 1919 by returning survivors. Comprised mainly of prominent locals and landlords, it unofficially acted as a military government, focusing on resettlement, food supply, and education. The second entity emerged in the summer of 1920 when the Armenian Legion dissolved, and Kessab's volunteers returned home. Movses Shahbazian led a detachment of 40 guards and police as part of this military authority.

Union. These two bodies were led by two individuals, Doctor Avedis Injejikian, a kind and caring doctor, beloved by all and the chief of the liberation self-defense forces, the incomparable Dayi, Ovsia Saghdjian. The latter, with his charm and his 25-30 comrades, played a significant role during that period in Kessab by founding an orphanage furnished by the looted items and food from the Turkish villages. At that time, Kessab nominally fell under the French occupation and administration, but not a single French soldier or official appeared in Kessab, which was part of Syria in 1920, and hence Kessab had, de facto, an independent government.

In March 1920, in the vicinity of Kessab, Dayi and his friends arrested five to six Germans, who were fleeing to Turkey. No one in Kessab was able to understand them since no one knew any German. Hearing that I was schooled in a German orphanage during the genocide, they took me to Kessab as an interpreter. However, when I entered the Fedayeen's station and met with Dayi, I trembled first because Dayi was wearing a pair of jumpsuit pants, long boots, and a cloak made of goat's hair. On the cloak were a few crisscrossing bullet-belts; on his belt a Parabellum pistol and a long dagger; a short French-made Martin rifle on his shoulder in addition to a huge pelt hat on his head. That was how I saw Dayi the first time. The four or five friends surrounding him had nearly identical frightening appearances.

Since I didn't know why I was summoned, fear took hold of me. Dayi noticed this and with a gentle tone, speaking with a childlike stammer, addressed me as an old friend. He said, "My son, don't be scared, I used to be your father's friend. I called for you to meet you; you have grown." As he went on, it was impossible to imagine what a kind voice would emit from such a terrorizing appearance. So, I took heart. After asking how my mother and I were doing, he asked me if I really knew German. I said that I did, that I had learned when I was in the German orphanage.

"You know, we have seized some worthless Germans," Dayi said, "and we would like to know who they are, where are they heading, etc. Can you interpret for us?"

I said I will do my best to interpret what I understand.

And so, they brought in the four or five young Germans in tattered clothes. They were all handsome with sunburned cheeks and proud stances.

I translated the questions and the answers of each as much as I could understand — I mean their names, surnames, ages, which army they belonged to, where they had come from, and where they were going. With that information, it became clear that after the cease fire and being running and hiding for a long time (two years), they were running from one place to another and wanted to go to Turkey by way of the mountains of Kessab. They begged a lot for their captors not to hand them over to the French.

Dayi gave me a present in return for the task I accomplished and sent me home. Later I learned that the German prisoners were handed over to the French authorities in Latakia, according to the previous agreements made between Kessab authority (an interim Kessab government as a result of anarchy) and the French.

This is how the winter and spring of 1920 passed by for me.

In the summer when the harvesting season began, my mother and Uncle Garabet took me with them to the wheat fields. In the evening, they loaded a bundle of wheat stalks on my back to carry home. Since I was not used to working in the fields, I felt terribly exhausted, particularly when the wheat stalk bundle became untied with each step I took, and I was forced to sit down so my mother or my uncle would reorganize them.

For a few days, awkward backbreaking labor made me think of voluntarily leaving Kessab. I told my mother that I didn't want to stay in Kessab any longer and would like to go to Beirut with Matisents Hagop, one of my cousins from the same generation, Uncle Serop's son. At that time, he worked in Beirut with the Sarafians as a photographer, and he was vacationing in Karadouran. Apparently that was what Uncle Garabet had wanted all along. Realizing that I was not inclined for farm work, he had decided to make me suffer so I would get disgusted and go to the city to try my luck.

That summer we rebuilt our paternal house, where I took part as a laborer. In August, when the renovation of the house was nearly complete, I resided there for only a week. Uncle Garabet gave me two Ottoman gold coins and I, together with Cousin Hagop and other travelers, set sail in a schooner from the shores of Karadouran south to Beirut. As soon as I boarded the schooner, my maternal grandfather, George Kairchian, came to bid me farewell. He, too, gave me half an Ottoman gold coin as pocket money.

During that period, Syria and Lebanon were under the military occupation of the French. In order to move from one city to another, you had to have a special permit and identity card. But in Kessab not a single French office existed, so I traveled with the Kessab National Union Identity Card, issued by the locals who advised me that it would be acceptable to the French.

When the schooner left Karadouran seashore,[5] the air was warm with a mild breeze. When we arrived in open seas, wind developed and in a couple of hours became quite a bit stronger. The waters became choppy as we sailed by Latakia. We were just beyond the tiny island of Rouwad, opposite the city of Tartus and close to the city of Tripoli, when the waves became so fierce that the boat's rudder broke. The captain worked hard to get us to Tripoli, but seeing it was impossible returned to the tiny island of Rouwad, where we took shelter.

Tartus, Syria

Realizing that the stormy seas may last for days, the captain, using local rowboats, took us to the city of Tartus. From there we could drive on to Beirut by car (89 miles, 143 kilometers away). He promised he would get our things to Beirut when the waves died down. Around 10 of us rented a 1919 Ford pickup truck and left for Beirut.[6] A few days later,

5 Karadouran seashore was a major link to the outside world from the 17th to the 20th centuries. (H. Tcholakian)

6 Before the Genocide, the Armenian community in Beirut lived near St. Nishan Church. Kessab students attended the American University of Beirut's medical school. After the ceasefire, many of these students moved to Beirut, primarily settling in the Zeytuniyeh District.

the schooner with our belongings arrived in Beirut. My possessions consisted of the mattress from the village of Ordou, my blanket also from Ordou, and a few pieces of clothing.

Beirut, 1940s

Beirut, 1958, Lucullus Restaurant named after Roman General Locullus.
(See World History Encyclopedia, Locullus and Tigranes the Great)

Chapter 12
EMIGRANT

Upon our arrival in Beirut, my cousin went to Lodging House shelter, owned and operated by the Near East Relief benevolent organization (USA) and the Armenian General Benevolent Union (AGBU). This was a building where Armenian orphans who earned money would stay. They were obliged to pay half their salaries to the shelter no matter what their income and, in return, the Lodging House paid for their food, their sleeping accommodations, and their laundry. The rest was dealt with by the administration of the shelter.

I was new to the city. Since I neither had a job nor an income, I did not qualify to get admitted into the Lodging House, despite having pleaded many times. Therefore, from day one, I had problems. I was a stranger to the city, abandoned, and helpless. Where and how was I supposed to live with the only two Ottoman pounds I had? On the first night, I stayed in a very modest hotel, and the next day I crisscrossed the city, looking for employment. As I was passing by the Catholic cemetery in the Zeytunieh District, I overheard someone speaking in the Kessab dialect, so I went to him.

His name was Topalian, an elderly man and the security guard of the cemetery. He lived there as well with his wife in a room. When he realized I was a native of Karadouran, and that I had no shelter, he invited me to stay with them. I didn't wait for him to repeat his offer a second time. I immediately got my things from the hotel and brought them to the Topalian's house. Imagine a 15-year-old boy living in a cemetery. Conditions forced me to live there, and I was grateful.

I was focused on getting a job as soon as possible so that I could qualify to live in the Lodging House. For the next 15 to 20 days, I went from one shop to another, from one office to another, wandering continuously, offering my service — for any kind of work — so that I could earn something and move to the Lodging House. However, there weren't any jobs offered. Wherever I would go, they'd look me over and would ask if I had a trade and what I could do. When they found out I had no trade and that I was a mere schoolboy, they would reject me.

One day, after wandering for 21 days without results, I fearlessly walked into the office of the representative of General Motors Company and asked to see the office manager. One of the workers tried to stop me, but hearing my pleading voice the manager allowed me to come in. That man's charm and pleasing face and his gentle and kind attitude left good impressions on me. It turned out that he was a Christian Lebanese American, Fouad Nasrallah.

With my broken English and Arabic, I boldly explained to him that I was an orphan and a stranger to Beirut. I had been wandering the streets for 21 days in search of a job. Soon whatever savings I had left was going to end. I implored him to give me a job in their office so that I could give half of my salary to the Near East Relief shelter and be admitted there. When he heard that I was living in the cemetery facing his office, he empathized with my situation and started questioning my abilities.

After doing a little test, he noticed that I knew how to read and write both in English and Arabic. He told me that from this day forward I would be the office boy of the company. My duty would be to clean the office every morning, organize all the papers in the drawers — it was a car and car-parts dealership. I had to organize the auto parts in the drawers, take letters to and from the post office, and go to different places as needed. He asked me if I would be able to do these tasks. I said I could. Then with enthusiasm, I started to put everything in order and polish the floor.

The next day, my first full day, he sent me to the post office twice. I didn't even know where it was. When he asked me if I knew where the post office was, I lied and said that I did, fearing that if I had said no, he would have not hired me. I ran out and started asking passersby where the post office was. I found it. I did the same with the addresses of all the customers according to whatever undertaking they would send me for. He was going to pay me three Syrian liras per month in return for my services. During those days, two Syrian pounds made one British sterling. I was saved.

A few days later my manager appeared to be satisfied with my work, but I knew that my money would be gone before payday. I only had a few days' worth of finances. Payday was too far away. I kept thinking, "What should I do? How to survive in the meantime?"

One morning as I was not being myself or energetically doing my job, Mr. Nasrallah, noticing how preoccupied I was, approached me and asked if I needed anything or if I were feeling unwell. With a heavy heart, tears started flowing. Upon his insistence, I shared my concern, saying that whatever money I had left was coming to an end and there were three more weeks before I would receive my salary. I asked if it were possible for him to write a letter to the shelter's administration mentioning my earnings. Would it be possible for him to advance me half of my salary so I could give it to the administration of the shelter, where I could live and be free from worry?

My employer, Mr. Nasrallah, with great empathy, agreed with my request. In the evening, with the one-and-a-half Syrian lira and his letter, I ran to the shelter, where I was immediately accepted. My joy was boundless. I went to the cemetery at once and thanked senior compatriot Topalian for his hospitality. I collected my belongings and moved to the shelter, where I had a place to sleep beside my cousin Hagop. I was free of the nightmare.

During the next months — September, October, and November 1920 — I worked quietly in that kind man's office. He increased my salary each month and at times would give me special gifts. During those few months, I lived frugally. I was even able to save nearly four sterling pounds. I did not have free time in the office. When I did not have anything to do, I would study with a book so that I would improve my English. My manager was very satisfied with this.

Having worked here for three months, I started pondering what my future would be as an office boy. I began recalling my past school years and yearned for my orphan life, where at least I was getting an education. I would remember Schneller's Orphanage, which was now in the hands of the British. I started thinking if it were possible to go to Jerusalem and try to get back in the orphanage to continue my studies.

I thought about this for a few weeks. I went into Mr. Nasrallah's office and timidly shared my ideas with him about resuming education. I asked if he could help me get a passport so I could go to Jerusalem to study. I told him that I had a married aunt near the Armenian monastery. I would stay there until I was able to go to school. Since he noticed that I had a genuine desire to continue my education, my manager said he would be happy to help me. He even praised my ambitions.

He wrote a note to Mr. Dikran Sarafian, who was a member of the then Beirut National Union and had ties with the Nansen[1] office. My manager asked him to prepare for me, on his behalf, a Nansen passport to go to Jerusalem. My passport was ready a week later. Mr. Nasrallah paid for and booked me a ticket on the Italian Lloyd Triestino Liner. He put me on board with his blessings.

The ship sailed in the evening and around 7 a.m. arrived at Haifa.[2] Carrying my mattress and a small bag for my clothes, I started walking on the wharf toward town. Sometimes I would ask about an Armenian. A little later, I met a man who was Armenian. He worked at the train station. His name was Papazian. I asked him to show me a modest hotel. When he realized my situation, he told me to follow him and entered a house.

The house did not look like a hotel. I asked him if this was a hotel. Mr. Papazian said, "No, this is my house and my family. Tonight, you are our guest. Tomorrow, I will put you on the train on your way to Jerusalem." He asked me if I had anywhere to stay in Jerusalem. I said that first I would go to my aunt's house and then would try to go to school, either at Schneller's German Orphanage or the seminary if I am accepted.

Mr. Papazian said that his three sons, Torkom, Missak, and Aram were tuition-paying boarding students of the seminary. My going there would be his chance to get a letter to his sons with some money. That evening, I was Mr. Papazian's guest. The next morning, after a night's sleep, he took me to the station. Since he was the stationmaster, he got me a free ticket and sent me off to Jerusalem. He gave me a letter with 50 Egyptian pounds to give to his sons.

1 Fridtjof Wedel-Jarlsberg Nansen (1861-1930), a true Armenophile, became interested in the Armenian Question at the end of the Hamidian Massacres (1894-1897). After WWI, he founded a network of philanthropic offices which supplied Nansen passports to Armenians, and others, including Jews and Assyrians. These passports were perhaps the only identifications Armenian refugees had. Most Armenians used these Nansen passports to immigrate to Europe, the US, and South America. These passport remained valid until 1950. (Hieronymi, Otto (2003). The Nansen Passport: A Tool of Freedom of Movement and of Protection, Refugee Survey Quarterly. Vol. 22, #1 [pp. 36-47]. https://academic.oup.com/rsq/article-abstract/22/1/36/1602978?redirectedFrom=fulltext.)

2 Haifa, a major Palestinian seaport, hosted Armenian refugees from Jordan after the ceasefire. These refugees helped revive old Armenian communities in Gaza, Ramle, Jaffa, and Haifa. After 1919, many Syrian and Lebanese Armenians moved to Palestine for job opportunities. During the British colonial period, Kessab Armenians found work, particularly in road building and construction.

The Old City of Jerusalem with Armenian Quarter

St. James Armenian Monastery, Jerusalem

When I got to the station at Jerusalem, I did not have any difficulty because I was familiar with the city. Carrying my belongings, I headed toward the Armenian Monastery and went to my aunt's house (one of the Monastery's civilian rental units). They were astonished to see me: how in the world had I gotten there? My aunt, who is three years my elder, had married at a very young age. She already had two children.

I arrived in Jerusalem during the first week of December 1920. After resting for a few days, I wanted to know about the Schneller Orphanage and learned that their education level was much lower than before. So I asked Mr. Reynolds, the principal of the British Saint George School, to accept me as a boarder free of charge. This is the same Mr. Reynolds who used to be the scout leader in the Armenian tent city of Port Said. He had sponsored five to six Suediya boys to be admitted to Saint George.

He recognized me at once as the youngest boy scout. "Sadly," he said, "the school doesn't have enough of a budget to admit another student for free. If you are able to find a benefactor who would be willing to pay half of your tuition, I would be willing to accept you as a boarder." He gave me some names of wealthy Armenians with whom to get in touch.

I was so thirsty for education. Without hesitation, I asked around and found the address of a wealthy Armenian, Paul Lazaros (Boghos Ghazarian), and went to his house. This wealthy man lived in a magnificent villa in the Baqaa District of Jerusalem near the Jerusalem Station. He had accumulated his wealth in India, working for a maharaja. It is said that the maharaja had left him a mythological wealth, and he had a large collection of artifacts. His wife was British, and they had a daughter.

I knocked on that door and asked for an audience. They let me in. I was in the presence of a respectable but stingy elderly man, to whom I told my life story in a concise way. I asked for the half tuition that Mr. Reynolds had wanted. I would take the responsibility of returning the money I would borrow with interest as soon as I graduate and start working. He was sympathetic, but he was not in a position to provide me the funds. He added it would be better if I applied to the Armenian Seminary. Disappointed by this man, I returned to my aunt's house.

Time was going by, and I was in a hurry to start school by whatever means. By attending a day school, I would be an economic burden to my aunt and her husband. I turned down their repeated offer for paying for a day school and decided to apply to the Armenian Seminary.[3] The Papazian brothers, to whom I had handed their father's letter with the funds at the seminary, suggested that I apply directly to His Holiness the Patriarch, Archbishop Yeghisheh Tourian,[4] a venerable, apostle-like personality. So I sat down to write my application letter. Although I had irregular Armenian schooling in Karadouran, Port Said, and the Haigazian School in Aleppo, I knew enough Armenian. But was my skill in the Armenian language worthy enough to write an application addressed to His Holiness?

Archbishop Yeghisheh Tourian

3 The Jarankavorats (Heritage in Arm.) School, located in the St. James Monastery in Jerusalem, was established in 1843. It is a boarding High School for students of Theology. The Monastery shut down during WWI and has been reopened since 1920.

4 A prolific writer and an ardent teacher, Yeghishe Tourian (February 23, 1860-April 27, 1930) was the Armenian Patriarch of Constantinople from 1909-1910. In 1921 he was elected Patriarch of Jerusalem. He is credited for having revitalized the Armenian School, Jarankavorats within the Armenian Patriarchate of Jerusalem. He remained in his post until 1929. He arranged for many young Armenian orphans to attend the school.

I thought it would be best if I first wrote my autobiography as a summary of my life, highlighting my thirst for education; that I would be a clergyman after I graduated, etc. I wrote, rewrote, edited five times, and then very carefully and as neatly as possible wrote the last version. A few days later, with this letter of application in hand, I presented myself at the Patriarchate.

Despite the fact I had done my best to be clean, neat, and tidy, the gatekeeper refused to let me in. Seeing my stubbornness, and that I had waited for more than an hour, he finally informed the patriarch that a young man insisted on seeing him and didn't want another person to hand him the application he was holding. The patriarch allowed me to come in. When I entered Archbishop Yeghisheh Tourian's office library in the patriarchate, I saw in front of me the benevolent gaze of an apostle-like and robust-framed venerable theologian.

Confused, I froze in the doorway. A soft, kind voice came out of that big-framed body as he said to me, "Come in, my son. What would you like from me?"

Baffled, I was tongue tied and couldn't utter a word. Approaching him, I kissed his extended right hand and handed him the application I was holding on to. On the envelope I had written in big letters "Application."

He generously ordered me to sit down in the chair facing him and began to carefully read my letter from beginning to end. My letter was quite long because I was describing my life story. When he finished reading, he gently raised his head and with a smile on his face asked me, "Have you written this narrative yourself?"

"Yes", I replied.

"Nobody helped you or corrected this petition?"

"No," I said and added, "I rewrote it four or five times and copied this sixth version."

He said, "It has been written with care. Maybe a man will come out of you, but I dislike your last paragraph, where you say that after graduation you would like to become a clergyman. At the age of 15, you can't decide a thing like that. You will only decide when you already have graduated school and get older."

I was waiting. After this introduction he hadn't said his decisive yes or no.

The Patriarch Father's continuous smile gave me hope. Upon reflecting for a while he said, "It seems you are a good boy, and if you work as hard as you have in composing your letter, you would reach somewhere. So now, I will write to the superintendent of the seminary to admit you to school after the Christmas Holy Days."

At once, I kissed his right hand with gratitude. Moved and with tears in my eyes, I waited with my heart palpitating until he finished his note to the superintendent of the seminary. In those times, Mesrob Supreme Archimandrite Nishanian was the superintendent. He later became the Patriarch of Jerusalem. With a happy disposition and tightly holding the letter that contained the realization of my future plans — getting education, education, and more education — I went to give the good news to my aunt.

Chapter 13
THE SEMINARY

As soon as the Christmas Holy Days ended, I went to see the superintendent of the seminary in January 1921. I was immediately accepted. A few days later, I was given the school uniform and all other clothes. After an exam, they placed me in the first grade. At that time, the seminary had two grades only. One of the grades was the equivalent of elementary sixth grade, and the other was the equivalent to the seventh grade. They put me in the sixth elementary.

Even though I had missed the first semester of the 1920-1921 academic year, with hard work I not only was able to learn what I had missed but, by the end of the school year, I was awarded the title of best student of my class for that year. There were 38 students total in both grades. Each grade had 18 to 20 students.

At that time, the following was the list of classes and teachers:

Classical Armenian Language	Yeghisheh Archbishop Tourian
Church History, 301 C.E.-1920	Papken Archbishop Guleserian
Theology	Bishop Aghavnouni
Armenian History and Literature	Dikran Kapikian
Science and Mathematics	Eolmezian
Church and National Patriotic Music	Krikor Chilinguirian
English	Deacon Guregh (later Archimandrite, Bishop, and Patriarch)
French	Deacon Aram (Mampre) Kalfaian (later Archimandrite, then Bishop, and now through 1958, Primate of the American Diocese)
Overseer	Priest Hovsep Der-Vartanian

During the second academic year of 1921-1922, I was a diligent student and was again the first in class. So I became spoiled and mischievous.

Kevork in the Armenian Seminary, Jerusalem, 1921-1923

The seminary students were under strict supervision. We were not allowed to go out by ourselves or in groups unless accompanied by a teacher or an overseer. Although it was absolutely forbidden to visit our relatives, they could visit us every two Sundays for half an hour only. They had to inform the administration beforehand. We were not even permitted to visit our relatives on holidays.

We would wake up early. After washing and getting dressed we were supposed to go to church and attend the divine service. Later at 7:30 a.m., we would have our breakfast. Our classes started at 8 a.m. The holidays were tiresome for us. We had to sing loudly for hours. Our voices had to be audible over the noise of the churchgoers, especially in the Church of St. Haroutiun (Resurrection). The same thing happened on Christmas Holy Day at the Cathedral of Bethlehem, where the divine liturgy of Christmas Eve would start at 10 p.m. and continue uninterrupted until 9 a.m. the next morning. Since we were too young, we would get tired and sometimes would sing sleeping standing up as if hypnotized in a trance. We would at times sing incorrectly, but Mr. Chilinguirian would poke us, and we would shout anything, causing laughter among the parishioners.

Bethlehem, The Church of Nativity

However, our summer vacation was magical. They would take us to the Monastery of Bethlehem. In addition, almost every day, they would take us to the surrounding villages on the outskirts of Jerusalem and on nature trip excursions. Most of the time, we would enjoy our lunch that we brought with us in raw nature or in lush green gardens. When we had money given to us by our relatives, we could purchase anything we desired outside of the monastery but not after getting inside the St. James Monastery courtyard. However, whenever we wanted to get something after the gates were locked at 8:30 p.m., two of my close friends, Levon Fabrikajian from Erzurum and Garabet Aghajanian from Jerusalem, would keep watch so that others wouldn't notice I was missing. I would climb down a rope that was previously set up by us in secret on the walls of the Church of the Hreshdakabed (Archangel), cautiously head to the market, get the necessary things, and return.

During the Easter Holy Days of 1923, an Armenian play was going to be staged in the Zion Movie Theater. Supreme Archimandrite Mesrob, the superintendent, was invited to attend with other clergymen. Three best friends, Levon Fabrikajian, Garabet Aghajanian, and I decided to go, too. We let our acquaintance from Erzurum, Mr. Sissag, get us three tickets in the last row of the theater and somehow got them to us in time. That evening, the gate of the monastery that was usually locked at 8:30 p.m. was going to stay open until midnight, allowing the resident clergymen and civilian staff of the monastery to attend the play as well.

Zion Movie Theater, Jerusalem

At around 8 p.m., like our classmates, we went to bed except that the three best friends went to bed fully dressed. A quarter of an hour later, the overseer, Mr. Der Vartanian, whose room was adjacent to our dorm room sleeping quarters, came in to check up on us. Then he went back to sleep. As soon as the bedroom lights were turned off, the three of us got out of bed, put on our coats, and pretended we were going to the communal bathhouse in the garden courtyard. We hid our coats in the bushes and proceeded toward the Monastery gate.

We were well-disguised. We pulled down our hats that were bought from outside the monastery, and we headed out. We suddenly noticed that the overseer, Der Vartanian, was walking right in front of us. Turning back was not an option. So I discreetly let my friends know that as soon as we found an unlit dark corner, we should swiftly bypass the overseer. As soon as we did that, we rushed to the theater before anyone could see us. Once inside, we sat hunchbacked in our assigned seats. To our surprise, we saw our relatives who were astonished to see us there and came up to us. Getting rid of one, another one would pop up. Finally my aunt came, and I made her understand that we had come without anyone's knowledge or permission. I asked her to prevent the rest of the relatives from approaching and visiting us.

Right after the play ended, we hit the road back. On our way, we thought of buying some roasted chickpeas, so we went to Bab el-Amad, which added another 30 minutes to our trip. When we got back, we saw that the Monastery gate was already shut. We were ready for everything, though. We had tied a rope from the wall of the Hreshdakgabed (Archangel) Church. The hanging end of rope was resting on the awning of an adjacent shop. One of us climbed on the shoulder of the other, grabbed the rope resting there, and we all climbed over the wall overlooking the seminary playground. Then very quietly and one by one, we tiptoed through the garden to get our coats and return to our bedroom, pretending as if we were just returning from the courtyard bathroom.

To our great surprise, our coats were not there. Slowly we went into the bedroom, got undressed, and turned down the blankets to go to sleep. On our pillows, we saw a note in the overseer's handwriting. It said we needed to show up in his office at 8 a.m. the next day. We panicked and whispered to each other that we were caught in the act.

Then we saw that one of our friends in the next bed was awake. He was sneering at us. We at once grabbed him at his throat and told him it was his doing, and he readily confessed that he had forged those notes. This friend of ours was great at imitating handwriting. He had replicated the overseer's handwriting so well that his forgery was indiscernible. The boy said this was his revenge for not inviting him with us.

We thought that we were in the clear — undetected.

Some five or six days after this incident, the overseer called all three of us and wanted to know where we were on the night of the play. We boldly told him that we were in bed and awake when he came in to check up on us. Let me mention that when we had left for the theater that night, we had positioned our pillows lengthwise on the bed, covering them with towels, supposedly to protect us from mosquitoes. We had done this to give the impression that we were under the covers when the overseer did his inspections.

He said that there were people in the theater who had seen us there. We denied these accusations wholeheartedly because the fear of expulsion was within us. A few days after that, the superintendent called us and asked the same questions. Once again we denied everything. He insisted persistently for us to at least explain how we had gotten out of the monastery. He added that if we confessed, he wouldn't punish us, but we had to deny everything.

It was only months later, our friend the French teacher, promising not to tell the superintendent, made me confess. He tried to close the subject. From then on, this French teacher became a close friend of mine. When he advanced to the status of priest (archimandrite), he helped me a lot. I am indebted to him and soon will write about him.

While I was in the seminary, I naturally wrote to my mother, brothers, and Uncle Garabet in Kessab every two to three weeks. My uncle used to write colorful letters. He would advise me to get a good education and become a good man. The superintendent opened any correspondence to and from families. The letters full of valuable advice pleased even the superintendent. He would say that I had a very educated and progressive-thinking uncle. I had never warned my uncle that his letters underwent inspection. My uncle would write letters every 15-20 days, as I did.

For a time, I hadn't received mail for two months. Worried, I would ask the superintendent if any mail had arrived for me from my uncle. He would say no. I became suspicious. I asked Deacon Aram, later Archbishop Mampre Kalfaian.

He said, "You didn't hear it from me, but there was a letter for you last week on the superintendent's desk. That same letter is in his desk's left drawer. It looks like he doesn't want to give it to you."

I went directly to the superintendent. When he told me I didn't have any mail, I told him there must be a mistake. I said, "I do have a letter, and it is in your left drawer."

First, he feigned surprise. Then, he opened the drawer and pretended to read the letter. He said it wasn't a good idea for me to read it.

"Since it is addressed to me, whether it contains good or bad contents, it belongs to me," I insisted. "You are under obligation to hand it to me."

Angered, he threw the letter to my face.

I took it and left the room. In the letter my uncle had written, "I heard you wanted to be ordained an archimandrite. Don't you dare. Just get your education. After you graduate, leave." I don't know how my uncle had heard about this, which was untrue. I had a long way ahead to finish school, and I had never been thinking about it. I could still hear His Holiness Patriarch Tourian's words regarding my petition, "My son, it is too early for you to think of becoming a clergyman. You can only make such a decision when you are more mature."

So that's why the superintendent did not want to give me the letter. He was afraid that my uncle's advice will confuse my future plans. From that day on, he and some members of the faculty, especially those subject to the superintendent and particularly the overseer, started showing me a cold shoulder. They started to punish me for the smallest wrongdoing or mischief.

Left: Kevork with Archbishop Mampre Kalfaian, Jerusalem circa 1945
Right: Kevork, baptism of niece Roubina, with his other Godchildren, Yaffa 1945

As a result, I rebelled at a very young age and became a more active mischief maker. Finally, I wrote to the superintendent that I wanted to leave school and handed in my written resignation. The former called me and said, "We gave you free food and education for two years. According to the Seminary regulations, you are obliged to serve in the monastery for a year as compensation. It is only fair, then you can drop out."

I told him that I would leave immediately without serving.

The superintendent threatened that he would make me do it with the help of the police.

There was one way I could leave the school: to be so misbehaved and impish that they would be compelled to expel me from school. So I started skipping class and communal meals; eating my food alone; fighting with teachers who argued with me. When all these were futile, I would leave the premises of the monastery without permission and go places. I would try my best to be back at exactly 3 p.m., when the boys would go to evening mass.

I wanted the superintendent to see me returning from outside the walls of the monastery. And one day, that is what happened. On this day, the superintendent came at 3 p.m. He told me in a harsh manner, "Where are you returning from?"

I said, "From outside."

"Get lost. Go back where you came from. Let me never see you again."

"Thank you so much," I replied. "When months back, I kindly asked you to let me go, you refused. Now my initially polite request was fulfilled by impolite means." I went straight to my aunt's house.

Chapter 14
LIFE'S TRAJECTORY

I intended on finding a position in an office and to self-educate myself. So I stayed with my aunt in Jerusalem for a month. I wasn't able to find a job. During the latest months, Deacon Aram was ordained as Archimandrite Mampre. He was sent to Jaffa as the officiating assistant superintendent of Armenian Church in Jaffa.

When I was at the school, I was one of Mampre's favorite students, so I wrote him a note to see if he could help me find a job. He advised me to come to Jaffa. Although I was among the top students learning English at school, it was not sufficient for me to qualify for a job in an office. However, from his circle of friends, His Excellency Aram introduced me to Mr. Antoin Kassar, who was both the chairman of the Prince Line[1] and represented all the shipping enterprises owned by the Khedive (sultan) of Egypt.[2] In order to gain some experience, I was supposed to work there for three months as an intern (with no pay). If, after this probationary period, I showed improvement, he promised to give me a salary.

During those three months, the kind Vartabed Mampre fed me. He arranged free lodging for me at the Greek monastery, since he was fluent in Greek and a friend of the principal of the Greek seminary. By tradition, the gates of the Greek monastery, like those of the Armenian seminary, locked at 8:30 p.m. As a result, from 8:30 p.m. until midnight, I would study and improve my English. And in Mr. Kassar's office, I was entrusted with the filing position, where I was given every opportunity to go over, read, and classify each document in their corresponding envelopes and files. This job was a very helpful experience for me.

1 The Prince Line shipping company was founded by James Knott. It was incorporated on February 28, 1895, with a fleet of 14 ships, which helped attract shippers to the Prince Line. The company operated regular liner services to the River Plate, West Indies, Levant, Greece, Egypt, and Syria.

2 The Khedives were viceroys of Egypt since the time of Mehmet Ali the Great, who was able to seize the country as his own fiefdom from the Ottoman sultan. His descendants ruled Egypt until the Egyptian Revolution by the Independent Officers group (Gamal Abdel Nasser) in 1952. (See *Encyclopedia Britannica/Mehmet Ali.*)

Gradually, I started practicing on the typewriter. In those set terms of my three-month internship, I showed great progress. In the fourth month, I was hired as a fully paid member of the staff, where I earned a salary of three Egyptian pounds.

In those years right after the war, life was expensive, and three Egyptian pounds did not amount to anything, but at least I wasn't hungry. My only possession was a khaki suit with a buttoned-up collar that I had brought with me from the seminary, a change of underwear, and socks. Therefore, Vartabed Mampre fed me one more month so that I could buy some change of clothing with my first salary.

Incessantly and without exception, I continued my private study sessions every night from 8:30 p.m. 'til midnight. In the office, too, I toiled and got everything done that either the manager or the staff would give me or allow me to do. I had a very kind supervisor by the name of George Halabi.

He always appreciated my work, even if I made some mistakes. He would never say, "It's bad," but "Very well done, my boy, only if you could write this sentence this way or that way would be better." Or he would say, "I think this word is written this way," and he would correct my mistakes, and let me rewrite it until he approved it.

With this kind encouragement, I was able to advance sufficiently within a year. In the first year, I was in a very tight economic situation. On my fifth month of employment, Mampre Kalfaian went to France to serve as the pastor of the Marseille Armenian community. I was left without his support, and I had to make do with three Egyptian pounds a month. There were times during the year that I didn't have breakfast in the morning. I wanted to buy a book or a copybook or a shirt with the money instead of spending it for breakfast. My lunch and dinner were very modest: bread with cheese or olives. And once or twice a week I could afford to go to a restaurant, courageously, to have some warm food to eat.

My economically tight situation continued for exactly one year. The next year, in January 1925, my salary increased to five Egyptian pounds, which significantly improved my quality of life. I was even able with half a pound to have private lessons with the local English clergymen in correspondence and accounting, which became very useful for my position.

My manager, Mr. Kassar, would always speak in French with me, and although I understood (I had learned it in school), I had not practiced it and would answer him in Arabic. One day he said, "My son, don't you know French?"

I said, "I studied enough to understand what you are saying. I have never practiced speaking it, but I promise that I will speak with you in acceptable French within a year."

He told me that I wouldn't be able to learn French that easily. It was impossible to be a fluent French speaker in a year. However, if by next New Year's Eve, I would be able to answer all his questions in French, he would double my salary. Thus, we wagered. I was certain that he made his promise to encourage me.

From that day on, my reading consisted of only French novels. At first, I read novels that I easily understood, then thicker volumes. I read them all aloud. Every day, and with no exceptions, I read aloud in my room from 8:30 p.m. until past midnight. In the office, I started speaking in French with the clerks and with some of the customers. Even if they spoke in Arabic with me, I would answer them in French, compelling them to speak in French with me. Even on the phone, I started answering the regular customers in French. Of course, for the first few months I misspoke French often. I had become the laughingstock of the assistants, but I didn't care and would stubbornly continue speaking in French.

During that whole year, I read more than 35 novels aloud. I read huge volumes of *Les Miserables, The Secrets of Paris, The Three Musketeers, The Count of Monte Cristo,* which were interesting as well as easily understood. Consequently by the end of the year, I spoke French fairly well. I noticed that since I hadn't learned French grammar, I made a lot of writing mistakes. The wager I had with Mr. Kassar was on spoken French and not on written French.

On the evening of December 31, 1925, on New Year's Eve, I went into Mr. Antoin Kassar's office and told him in French that I was ready to be tested on my French. He had almost forgotten our bet. But hearing my nearly immaculate French, he was pleased. He began asking me questions on shipment jobs in French, and I answered him slowly and focusing on my every word in understandable clear French.

He was so pleased that he delivered his wager. From that day onward, my salary doubled. As a result, I was freed of my economic hardship. During those difficult days, if I had written to my brother or uncle in Kessab, I was sure they were going to help me out. Being a novice young man, my pride would have been hurt if I had asked for an extended hand from my brother or uncle. Starting in 1926, the more I was successful at my work, the higher became my salary.

In the summer of 1928, I decided to go to my birthplace, Kessab, and see my mother, brothers, sisters, and relatives. I decided to take a vacation from May 15 to June 20. With a tidy sum of money with me, I left for Kessab.

I took my portable gramophone that I had bought that year with me so that we could have fun with friends. I had forgotten that our country during the months of May to June would be cold and rainy. I had assumed that it would be as warm as in Jaffa, I neither took with me an umbrella nor a coat. Instead, I had with me a full-length silk-wool windbreaker to keep the dust, dirt, and mud out of my clothes.

On the company's steamship, I traveled to Beirut, and from there continued immediately to Latakia by car. In 1928, the road to Kessab wasn't built for automobiles. Transportation was done on mules. As soon as I arrived in Latakia, I wired my brother to send me a muleteer to take me to Kessab. Since it was rainy, the mule man was late. After waiting in Latakia for two days, disgusted, I asked the innkeeper in what way could one travel to Kessab. He said that one could travel half the way by car then at the first Turkish village find a mule man to get to Kessab. I immediately decided to leave the next morning. In the morning, I rented a Ford car to take me 'til Guendel (about halfway to Kessab), where the uphill climb through forests to Kessab began on the condition that the driver of the Ford would get me a mule man from the nearby Turkish village.

It was a cloudy but hot day. As we approached Guendel, where our climb would begin, I noticed a muleteer wearing what resembled Kurdish attire, riding a mule heading toward Latakia. I immediately asked the driver to stop the car, and I asked the mule rider in Arabic where he was coming from. I suspected that he might be the one that my brother had sent me.

In broken Arabic, the man confidently and with pride told me that it wasn't any of my business where he was coming from.

I explained to him that I was waiting for a mule man from Kessab, and that's why I was asking him.

Then in the Kessab dialect he said, "Don't tell me you are that youngster from the Manjikian's."

So I knew that he was the mule man my brother had hired. His name was Hagop Sarkissian, the father of Vartabed Karekin,[3] one of the friars of the Catholicosate of the Holy See of Cilicia.

Catholicos Karekin I of All Armenians with his father Hagop Sarkissian and family members

Hagop was blessed with a sense of humor. He dismounted the mule, and after exchanging hello and God's greetings said, "Where are you heading in this rain? It would be best if we returned to Latakia. When the sky opens up, I will take you to Kessab, especially since neither I nor the mule have food to eat, and we have a long way to go still. I am afraid that you will get soaked and stay hungry on the way," and other advice.

But I was not inclined to go back to Latakia, especially since we were halfway there already by car, and urged him to turn back and take me to Kessab.

He said, "You don't have a raincoat or a coat on. Did you think this was Jaffa? Hey, if you start walking in the mud, your shoes will be stuck in the mud. Stop this stubbornness, and let's go back to Latakia."

It was impossible to convince me otherwise. Obligated, he tied my suitcase on one side of the mule and my gramophone on the other. He seated me on the mule. After paying the car driver and sending him off, we headed toward the mountain forests.

3 Archimandrite Karekin Sarkissian(1932-1999) later became Catholicos Karekin II of the Holy See of Cilicia, in Antelias, Lebanon from 1983 to 1995.(The Catholicosate in Sis , in Cilicia, southern Turkey Kozan (Trk.) was re-located because of the Armenian Genocide of 1915). The Holy See of Etchmiadzin in the Republic of Armenia, subsequently elected Karekin II as Karekin I, Catholicos of All Armenians, from 1995 to 1999.

We had covered only a short distance when my legs and backside started to ache because I wasn't used to riding. I wanted to walk a little. Hagop said, "Try it, but I fear that you will leave your shoes behind as a gift to the mud."

The rain had truly muddied the mountain trail. Every time I attempted to take a step, my feet would get out of my shoes which were heavy with mud. Laughing, Hagop lifted me back up on the mule for a second time. As we continued the uphill climb, the drizzle turned into a downpour. It rained this way for over an hour. Although Hagop was wearing a cloak made of goat's hair and knee-high rural red leather rain boots, both of us were soaked to the bones in that heavy rain.

It was impossible to reach Kessab in this rain. Hagop began to drive the mule faster so we could find shelter in the first Turkish home we saw. In spite of our drenched appearance, Hagop humored me once again by saying, "Hey, Manjikian boy, if the villagers refuse to give us shelter or food this evening, be warned that both of us will either die of hunger or catch pneumonia."

Indeed, for practical reasons that morning I had left with a light breakfast, without taking anything with me, hoping we will arrive early for a Kessab meal. Around four in the afternoon, I was feeling very hungry. At a distance, we saw a Turkish village on the hillside. We arrived at its confines around 5 p.m. It seemed all the village dogs were waiting to attack us. Luckily, I was on the mule, and Hagop could defend himself with a shepherd's cane.

Hagop implored me, "Whatever I tell the villagers, you must nod in agreement. Say yes or else we will stay hungry. If the village *agha* (leader, mayor) welcomes us as overnight guests, my aim is to play a trick on him so he will feed us and provide warm beds. Thus, whatever lies I tell, don't say anything but yes."

When we got to the first house, Hagop asked where the house of the *moukhtar* (head of the village) was. As luck would have it, it was Hassan Agha's, the mokhtar's house. After exchanging traditional greetings, invoking God's name in Turkish, Hagop continued. "Hassan Agha, I am taking this young agha to Kessab. He comes from a faraway country. We were caught in the rain, and it is impossible to continue. We ask you to welcome us at your home tonight."

Hassan Agha said, "Welcome, a thousand welcomes, a guest is a gift of

God," and according to village hospitality he invited us in. Immediately, he ordered his wives (he had several), "*Ablas* (wives, sisters), bring firewood and start the fire."

As soon as they lit the firewood stack, I asked to be excused to change my clothes, which were drenched. And in their presence, I opened my suitcase, and I took out underwear, shirts, etc., for both me and Hagop. We quickly changed and warmed our frozen bodies near the fire. And we hung our wet clothes near the hearth to dry.

When we sat down, Hassan Agha asked who I was. And, as Hagop had prepared me, he untied his sack of lies and said that I was the director of the British Bank in Palestine and that I was very educated, with a big salary, and endowed with this and that talent. I was barely able to suppress my laughter, but I kept my composure and presented myself matching the stature that Hagop had invented. Hassan Agha asked me whose son I was in Kessab.

Hagop then said that I was Manjikian Yessayi's grandson — in reality, Manjikian Yessayi was my grandfather's brother, whom almost every agha in the neighboring villages knew. He was mentioned above, as well.

Hearing this, the man became very happy and said, "Manjik Yessayi was a good friend of mine. He was the agha of the village of Karadouran. We visited him. When he came to visit us, we hosted him like this, and so I am honored to host the director of the British Bank, the grandson of Manjik Aysa ..." he said, along with other polite welcoming words.

But I was going to faint of hunger and said to Hagop, "Hey, Hagop, all this talk and these polite stories are making us hungrier. It would be great if you can find a way that they can give us a piece of bread. Otherwise, we are in trouble."

Hagop said, "Hey, be a little patient because the more I exaggerate, the more likely we are to get a royal meal and bedding."

In the meantime, the ablas were already busy preparing the food. A little later they brought in a small tray filled with a few pieces of bread, cheese, olives... and a bottle of araq.

"Oh! Let your house be doomed." Then I asked Hagop, "What am I going to do with araq on an empty stomach?"

He said, "You eat the *mezze* (appetizers), I'll drink the araq."

We had hardly drunk a glass of araq when Hassan Agha saw my gramophone.

"What's that?"

"It's called a gramophone," I told him.

In these villages, people had not seen one nor heard of it. Naturally, he was curious.

"It's a box that sings," I said.

"Does it also sing in Turkish?"

"Of course it does."

"Then make it sing."

Luckily, I had bought along with Armenian records some very good music in Turkish as well. When I put the first record on the gramophone, which was a *ghazal,*[4] the people were agape. The women with veiled faces near the doorway began to come nearer to listen to the inconceivable small box that sang Turkish on its own, which was so melodious. Hassan Agha was so taken with the songs that unselfconsciously "Allah, Allah" would flow from his mouth.

Moreover, they forgot about the supper. Inwardly, I started cursing Hagop profusely, the gramophone, and Hassan Agha, too. I gently poked Hagop and told him in the Kessab dialect, "Hey, Hagop, enough! I am dying of hunger. Find a way for them to bring the food quickly."

A while later, Hagop told Hassan Agha, "Agha, you know, these novice youngsters can't drink araq without eating any food. They are *a-la-franga* (French or people of the Western Hemisphere), and they only drink with their food. Forgive us, but would you ask them to bring the food now? It would be best for the Agha's health."

Hasan Agha said, "Of course, of course! Excuse us, *effendi* (title of honor), I never thought about that..." Calling to the ablas, he ordered them to bring in the supper. And what did they not bring! Fried chicken, crushed wheat pilaf, yogurt, cheese, butter, honey, and all the village food goodness. I don't know if this was in honor of Manjik Yessayi or for his grandson, who is the director of the British bank, or for the singing box, the gramophone? Whoever it was for, we were famished, like hungry wolves. I was eating slowly, against my will, to mask my hunger. But I wished I were eating faster. Naturally, as Hagop directed, I also drank the araq with the food to show that this was our custom.

4 A short poem consisting of rhyming couplets, rooted in classical Arabic poetry. Almost all ghazals are less than 15 couplets. They acquired musical form in the eighteenth and nineteenth centuries. With the development of recording and film industries, ghazal music became even more popular.

As soon as supper was over, I continued playing Turkish records. Not only was the house filled with its family members, but it looked like the entire village had come to the Hassan Agha's living room to listen to that wild animal. Being under the influence of the araq, the fire in the room, and the presence of the people breathing, the room was marvellously warm. My eyes were heavy with the fatigue of the day, a full stomach, and the effect of the araq.

Hagop would always poke me saying, "Hey, it's embarrassing. Be patient for a little while longer."

Being out of patience, I asked him to tell Agha to excuse me so I could get some sleep and, if they wished, they could play the gramophone in another room all night long.

The Agha looked at Hagop. "What does the effendi want?"

Hagop said, "Pardon us, Hassan Agha. The effendi is very tired and, since we are traveling tomorrow, he wants your permission to sleep. You know, Hassan Agha, we cannot get enough of your company. If God wishes for you to come with us, I hope you will come with us, and Manjik Aysa's grandson will have the honor to show you the same hospitality."

Hassan Agha said, "Of course, of course. How did I not think that the effendi would be so tired?" He subtly made the guests understand, and the crowd left.

Against their wishes, people had to disperse because our sleeping area was the living room itself. Hasan Agha called out, "Abla, bring the mattresses and lay them on the floor for the effendis."

Truly, the ablas brought two mattresses, put them on top of the other for me. They gave me a clean woollen blanket. For Hagop they had only one mattress with a woolen blanket. Wishing us a good night they went to their rooms so we could go to sleep.

Hagop said, "Hey, boy, if I hadn't inflated your stature as I did, you wouldn't have had this festive food nor this magnificent mattress, and we would have both died of pneumonia."

I exploded with laughter, which I was not able to hold onto any longer. I asked, "How did you come up with the Inguiliz Bankayi Moudir title and the grandson of Manjik Aysa?"

He said, "Hey, if it wasn't George Manjikian (Kevork's grandfather), let it be Manjik Aysa. He is your grandfather as well and well known in this area. If I had said you were a simple clerk, how much would have they given you...? Look, I did all that buffoonery, and now you have received the best portion! They gave you two mattresses, and me only one." Hagop reminded me that in the morning I must perform my role as agha with excellence, "Thus, when you say goodbye to Hasan Agha, jiggle the *mejids* (coins) in your pocket, then put them in his palm. I am certain he will refuse any kind of money, but you insist — and let him not take it."

Joking this way, we lay down on our soft mattresses and slept majestically. In fact, that comfortable mattress saved us from getting sick. In the morning, after the sun rose, we got dressed and went on our way. Before we hit the mountain trail, I showed my deepest gratitude to Hassan Agha in my broken Turkish and when saying goodbye, I put in his hand a heap of mejides. Seeing this, he got angry and said, "What is this, effendi? We were honored to be your host. It is shameful to accept money."

I said, "The money is not for you, Hassan Aga. The money is to buy some gifts from me for your children," but he adamantly refused as Hagop had predicted. Then Abla handed a parcel to Hagop, explaining that it was our breakfast, and we could eat it on the road. So their overnight welcome had been extended to breakfast on the road. It was a bright and sunny morning. Sitting on the mule and then thanking them once again, we headed to the trail in the forest.

At around 8 a.m., we came to a spring in the forest. We were halfway to Kessab. We sat and opened the breakfast parcel that Hassan Agha had given us. In it were boiled eggs, cheese, and honey. After having eaten our sumptuous breakfast beside the spring, we continued our way and got to Kessab around noon.

After an absence of eight long years, I again set foot on my native soil. What joy and happiness it was for me. I looked all around, and my gaze could not take it all in.

After having coffee at Hagop's house, we headed to Karadouran, to my ancestral village. It looked like those who had seen us in Kessab township had already let my family know. Half an hour away from arrival, I saw a crowd of young men, who were moving toward us with their guns firing in the air. My older brother, Hovsep, and my younger brother, Nishan, who was 19 years old, were among them. All my relatives and the entire village were there to greet me and bid me warm welcome. After all, I had been away for so long. I couldn't find words to describe their happiness and my joy.

I had grown up. I was almost 23 years old. The others, whom I saw last as children, had become young men and women. I saw new ones who had been born and had grown up after I had left. The Manjikian families had returned to their pre-April, pre-genocide numbers in population. The houses were rebuilt, the gardens and fields were cultivated with care. The whole village, like before, was full of livestock. In short, the presence of Armenian artisanship was alive and could be felt everywhere.

For days, relatives and acquaintances from nearby villages would come in endless rows to bid me welcome, as was the village custom. And almost every day, every relative would invite me to their house. With the young people, we would go to pilgrimage sights and beside mountain springs we would organize picnic feasts and *madaghs*[5] (offerings). During each of those 20 days, I had a fantastic and unforgettable time in Karadouran. When I was ready to return to Jaffa, I suggested my mother let my younger sister, Zabel, 14, come with me. "She could help me around the house, and I would be able to send her to school."

Sara, Kevork and Zabel in 1928

5 Sacrificial lamb (or goat); Armenian tradition dictated sacrificing an animal to feed a visiting guest.

My mother agreed. At the end of June 1928, with my sister for company, I returned to work in Jaffa. I worked with Mr. Antoin Kassar until 1933, earning a higher salary in a more important position. At 25, I decided to get married and start a family. Friends suggested that I meet with Miss Yeghisapet Aluzian from Afion-Karahisar. She was doubly orphaned, having lost both parents. At that time, she was studying midwifery in the Jerusalem State Hospital. A few years before that, she had received her nursing degree from the C.M.C. missionary hospital in Gaza.[6]

Al-Ahli Arab Baptist Hospital, in Gaza, 1999 photo credit Bob Ellis.[7]

Since I didn't know anyone who could go to ask her hand in marriage (according to the prevailing Armenian customs then), I made up an excuse to go to the hospital and, using a pretext, was able to see her. We exchanged some small talk. I liked her. Later in Jaffa, I wrote her a letter, saying I wished to ask her hand in marriage. When she did not answer, I went back in person, on a Sunday to repeat my marriage proposal. The young lady alleged she wanted to continue her education.

I told her that was not an obstacle and that we can get married after she gets her diploma — on condition that in the meantime we get engaged.

Apparently, she wanted to ask around about me so she wanted me to

6 The Church Missionary Society (CMS, later known as CMC) in the Middle East and North Africa operated through branch organizations, such as the Mediterranean Mission (for countries bordering on the Mediterranean), with the mission extending to Palestine (Jerusalem, Gaza, Haifa, Nazareth, Nablus,and Transjordan).

7 It was destroied On the morning of Palm Sunday April 2025 by Israel Defense Feces (IDF). UNZ Review, Ilana Mercer, April 23, 2025 (https://www.unz.com/imercer/genocides-back/)

give her a month, when she will give her final answer.

I gladly obliged.

Since as an orphan she didn't have anyone who could help her find out some information about me, she decided to see my employer, Mr. Kassar, and inquire. All of this was revealed to me after we got married. My future wife had come to Jaffa, and without seeing me, had gone directly to Mr. Kassar's residence, which was in an orange grove situated on the outskirts of Jaffa. She asked to see Mr. Kassar, one of the wealthiest and cultivated personalities in Jaffa. He was a native of Malta and had one daughter.

After the usual greetings, Mr. Kassar invited Yeghisapet inside the house and asked her the purpose of her visit. Yeghisapet told him that she was an orphan on both sides of her family, a certified nurse, and presently studying midwifery in the state hospital.

Without further ado, she asked, "If you had wanted to give your only daughter in marriage, would you have wished for her to be miserable and unhappy? Hence, since I don't have anyone, and since Kevork Manjikian, who works for you, asked for my hand in marriage, I thought that you would know him the most as he had been working for you for many years. So I wanted your honest opinion about that young man in order to make up my mind and not be unhappy in the future."

As Mr. Kassar was telling me later, her question moved him. After thinking long and hard, he answered, "My daughter, I have raised Kevork, and he has become a man in my presence. He is clever and witty. It may be that he doesn't earn a dazzling salary, but I am sure that he can make his future wife happy. I recommend you accept his proposal. If you do, like a daughter of mine, I will walk you down the aisle on your wedding day."

I was surprised when I heard from Yeghisapet before the one month was up. She wrote that she accepted. On December 31, 1930, we got engaged. After getting her midwifery certificate, she went to Amman as the nursing director in Mr. Purnell's hospital. After having stayed engaged for one and a half years, we got married on June 12, 1932. For the length of our 27 years of marriage — as I am writing this in 1958 — we have lived peacefully and happily without rancor. We have only had one misfortune: not being able to have children.

Kevork and Yeghisapet

During my employment in Jaffa, I also had a very fruitful public life. In April 1925, I founded, with a few friends, the Haygashen Armenian Educational Union. As far as I can remember, the members were Nigoghos Nigoghosian, Vosgan Sahagian, Vartivar Sarkissian, Nigoghos Kashkashian, Levon Alteparmakian, Apkar Gazmararian, and Kevork Manjikian. At the first opportunity, because we didn't have a club yet, we created a library for the union, in a corner of Mr. Vosgan Sahagian's shop. The first 100 books were donated by friends and acquaintances.

With my sustained efforts, the union was officially registered by the ruling British authorities. A few years later we formed our own association, and the number of the members sometimes increased to 120. The Haigashen Union from 1925 until the present (1958) still exists in Jaffa. It has had a fruitful life, celebrating every year, without exception, all our national holidays. It has given lectures, performances, concerts, and evening classes. It had athletic and football teams and a scout association. It has been a place for family and youth compatriotic gatherings, keeping the Armenian traditional values alive.

I am now an honorary member of the Haigashen Union along with being one of its founding members. For the duration of my life in Jaffa, I was a member of the administration of the Union and many times had been its chairman of the board.

In July 1928, during the celebration ceremony of the Invasion of Khanasor,[1] I became a baptized member of the Armenian Revolutionary Federation (ARF). Vahan Navasartian, Hamasdegh, and Onnig Majarian, who came to Jaffa for this celebration as speakers, were my ARF godfathers (during the ritual of a secular baptism of an Armenian joining the ARF party). Since 1928, I have been a member of the ARF and will remain so until my death. In Palestine I have taken up various roles within a local ARF organization: a group leader, subcommittee chair, a member of the committee. I have served my beloved political party with my humble abilities. But in 1948, during the sad expulsion of Arab Palestinians from Palestine, a large number from the Armenian community there were also forced to migrate alongside the Arab population. Only 10 percent of the Armenian community was left in Israel.

Haygashen Armenian Educational Union, Jaffa, Palestine

1 One of the successful military operations organized by the ARF to punish a Kurdish tribe that was harassing Armenian villagers for a long time. (Dasnabedian, Hrach [1990]. History of the Armenian Revolutionary Federation, Dashnaktsutiun, 1890-1924. [p. 50]. Oemme Edizioni.)

I continued my position in Jaffa as the highest position in the local office for the shipping company Prince Line until the end of 1939 when, because of the war (World War II), ships did not harbor at Jaffa. In the beginning of 1940, the company sent me to Haifa as the company director for the Haifa branch, where I remained until the end of 1940. Then I officially left my position when ships stopped harboring at the Haifa harbor. Once again, I returned to Jaffa, where I had a small temporary position until the end of August 1941.

In September 1941, I was summoned to work in Jerusalem with the United Kingdom Commercial Corporation (UKCC) as the shipping and trade operations specialist, which came with the title of vice president and a high salary. The UKCC was the trading branch of the British War Ministry in the Middle East. Its mission was not only to look after the food supply of all of the Middle East but to also buy all those commodities — no matter if they had to be tossed in the sea to prevent their purchase by the German enemy. In other words, it was the economic blockade of Germany. So I diligently directed this company as its vice president for four years until September 1945. Then the War Ministry awarded me a written letter of commendation.

Chapter 15
WITH ROUPEN DER MINASSIAN

While I was working for UK Commercial Corporation in Jerusalem, the British authorities, during the battle El Alamein,[1] whisked the illustrious leader Roupen Der Minassian[2] out of Egypt and brought him safely to Jerusalem. Giving precedence to my wish and request, Comrade Roupen Pasha and his wife lived in my house for three years. These were the happiest years of my life. For myself and my wife, Roupen became our father figure. We spent evenings compelling him to tell us of his experience as a revolutionary. During the period he stayed with us, he would often be busy typing the manuscript for his book, *Memoirs of an Armenian Revolutionary*. From this manuscript, he recounted different episodes that will forever remain in my memory.

I would like to tell you a few episodes from those dramatic stories, in memoriam to the one-of-a-kind — incomparable, grand, charismatic — revolutionary, who knew how to immortalize his humble friends and not so much himself. Usually Yeghisapet and I would take advantage of those moments when he was in a receptive mood or when he wanted to shed further light on our ideas. He had boundless love for his friends who had died and were heroes. When he spoke about one of them, even if the story was an amusing one, his eyes would fill with tears. Let me tell you a few episodes from Comrade Roupen's life, which I heard from him or witnessed first-hand myself.

1 Al 'Alamein, a desert post on the shore of the Mediterranean, 150 miles northwest of Cairo, was a battleground during World War II. German commander General Rommel was desperate to take the post and occupy Egypt and the Suez Canal. The Allied Forces Commander Gen. Montgomery fought to stop their advance. Fearing that the Germans might win, British authorities in Egypt secured the transfer of different ethnic and political figures from Cairo. ARF representative Roupen Der Minassian was thus relocated to Jerusalem. (Bierman, J., Smith, C. War Without Hate: The Desert Campaign of 1940–1943. Penguin Books: 2004.) **As Kevork later told his nephew, Zaven Manjikian, the Jewish leadership was preparing two ships to vacate Palestine and move to south America, in case Egypt fell into German hands.**

2 Born in Akhalqalaki, Georgia, Roupen Der Minassian (1882-1951) was a figure in the Armenian liberation movement and the third Minister of War of the first Republic of Armenia. After the Sovietization of Armenia in 1920, he moved to Zankezur (Armenia), then to Iran and Paris. In the Diaspora, he remained one of the prominent ARF figures. A major work of his, *The Memoirs of a Revolutionary,* in seven volumes was published, beginning in 1952; a second edition added Volume 8 published in Beirut, 1979. His closeness with Kevork Manjikian most probably played a role in Karadouran, naming its ARF club after Roupen Der Minassian. Also, Roupen and his family came to Kessab in the summer of 1947 and lived at Ovsia (Dayi) Saghdjian's home. He was, on one occasion, a guest at Hovsep's, Kevork's brother's house.

Roupen Der Minassian, 1882-1951

***

Roupen did not attend too many meetings and gatherings. One day when he had recently arrived in Jerusalem, and was not staying with us yet, we invited him to speak in one of our ARF group meetings. He did not refuse. The meeting took place in our house. To honor him, the comrades stood in rows on both sides of our entrance, as honor guards, so that he would pass through the middle. After the speech ended, the comrades stood in the same way as he departed.

That particular day, an orphaned school mate and close friend of my wife's, Siranoush Der Vartanian, was visiting us. The only things she recalled about her father were that he was a revolutionary and that his name was Aram. She had approached numerous other well-known revolutionaries about her father, but no one knew anything about him.

"Mr. Roupen was also a famous revolutionary and has operated in the Motherland, near Mush," Yeghisapet told Siranoush, "so wait for the meeting to end. As Roupen leaves, ask him; perhaps he knows something about your father."

Kevork's Jerusalem home, where Roupen Der Minassian and his wife lived during World War II; engagement ceremony of Vartouhie Seferian, Kevork's niece, 1945

The indoor honor guards formed rows to let Comrade Roupen pass through. As he turned to shake my wife's hand goodnight, he noticed the young lady beside her. His face immediately turned white and asked who she was. Siranoush for some reason became tongue-tied and was unable to speak.

"This lady is my friend," my wife intervened. "Presumably her father was a well-known freedom fighter in the Moush Dstrict. She wanted to ask if you knew anything about him."

"My dear girl, what is your name?" Roupen softly asked.

"Siranoush Der Vartanian."

When Roupen heard "Der Vartanian," Roupen froze, as if lightening had struck him. "Can you recall your father's name?"

"Yes, it was Aram."

"And your uncle's name?"

"It was Haig."

Upon hearing this, poor Roupen crumbled. His legs gave way. This giant of a freedom fighter, who showed no mercy toward his enemies, suddenly started to weep like a child. He hugged Siranoush and showered her cheeks with kisses and kept repeating, "Avrana Aram's daughter,[3] Avrana Aram's daughter!"

Avrana Aram's daughter Siranoush Der Vartanian

He was so overcome he couldn't stop the tears from flowing down on his face. We had to intervene. Only by asking him to sit down for a moment was poor Siranoush able to free herself from his grasp. After calming down a little, he said, "My dear girl, you look just like your father. Even if you hadn't told me your name, I could see in your face the presence of your father Avrana Aram, my kind, dear group leader, *Khempabed* (commander of a fedayeen cluster of up to 10 fighters) Avrana Aram. I am so emotional I won't be able to tell you anything now. I ask you to visit me tomorrow so we can talk about your father."

Then turning to my wife and I, he said, "Bow before the daughter of

3 Aram of Avran (*Avrana Aram in Armenian*) was one of the leaders of the Armenian fedayeen (freedom fighters) in Mush and Sassoon. He was in command of a cluster of up to 10 fedayeen when Roupen Der Minassian was active in Daron-Sassoon from 1904-1908, and again from 1913-1915. (*Memoirs of an Armenian Revolutionary*, Roupen. Vol. 7, 54-57, Second Edition: Beirut: 1979.)

national hero Avrana Aram. Know that her father and freedom fighters like him in Moush and Sassoon are national treasures to Armenians."

Thus, with tears still on his cheeks, and without looking back, Roupen passed through the honor-guard formation and walked out the front door. He had reduced us all to tears. Poor Siranoush remained sleepless all through the night. The next morning, she went to see Comrade Roupen and heard all the heroic stories of her father's life. During the Fedayeen national liberation battles (in which the freedom fighter code of honor was not to be taken prisoner), Avrana Aram had been wounded five or six times. Instead of falling in enemy hands, he preferred to commit suicide. But he was saved from being captured at every attempt.

ARF leader Vahan Papazian (Goms) and Armenian freedom fighter Mushegh Avedisian, AKA Khempabed Mushegh (Right)

In his final battle — when the Sassoun and Moush population retreated to Armenia, as freedom fighters Moushegh[4] and Goms (Vahan Papazian[5]) had written in their memoirs — Avrana Aram was wounded again. Unable to commit suicide, he pleaded with his comrades to put an end to his life so he would not land in the enemy's hands. That harsh duty fell

4 Mushegh is yet another heroic member of the Armenian national liberation struggle. He hailed from Khiyank village in Sassoon and was one of the surviving fedayeen leaders of Mush, Sassoon. He finally settled in Beirut after touring in Greece, Aleppo, and elsewhere.

5 "*Goms*" in Armenian literally means "the Count," a title associated with aristocracy. It was the nom de guerre of Armenian revolutionary Vahan Papazian, who represented the city of Van. Papazian served as a member of the Ottoman Parliament from Van following the 1908 constitutional revolution in the Ottoman Empire. (Humble Heroes [Khonarh Herosner]: Book A, Goms. [1949]. Beirut ARF Veterans' Foundation.)

to one of his relatives, who also was one of the freedom fighters in the Armenian liberation movement. Thus as he demanded, with a beloved bullet from his relative, Avrana Aram in order not to suffer the dishonor of being captured by the enemy died heroically for the liberation of his homeland and the people's freedom from Turkish rule.

Comrade Roupen had an astonishing and impressive memory recalling people. Whenever he met anyone, he would remember the person years later. He could even describe the place and occasion of the meeting.

***

One day in Jerusalem, as we were sitting drinking coffee in front of Vosgan Sahagian's tailor shop, Roupen suddenly noticed a man, around 35 years old; he shouted at him and said, "Young man, come here." That man — unfortunately I have forgotten his name — was Armenian and a resident of Jerusalem. When the man humbly came and greeted us, he suddenly asked him, "Aren't you the son of so-and-so?"

When the man said that he was — he was an ARF member— Roupen suddenly asked, "Did you know that your father was a traitor?"

At once, the man went pale and didn't know what to say.

Then softly Roupen said, "Come near me." He kissed the man and asked him to sit down beside him and added, "No, my son. Your father was a kind and true freedom fighter and my co-worker. Even though I wasn't aware that he had a son, you look like him. So I recognized you immediately. Your father was one of our friends in Kars. After the Ottoman Young Turk Revolution of 1908, when the constitution was restored, your father let my mother know about my planned return there, without realizing that I wanted to keep it as a surprise for her, and that's why I jokingly called him 'traitor.' Your father was a noble freedom fighter for national liberation. He became a victim of the Bolshevik May 1920 uprising[6] in the Republic of Armenia that was squashed by the Armenian Army. Your father is in the list of immortals who served the Armenian people and for the cause of the liberation of the fatherland."

***

Yeghisapet was the branch chairwoman of the Armenian Red Cross in Jerusalem. It seemed that in one of the administrative meetings some

6 Very first uprising against Bolshevik Communist Rule

critical remarks were made. She had returned home very angry and started grumbling and complaining. "It's not worth working for this community; they only know how to criticize; when it would be time to do one's job, they would disappear." Such were her complaints.

Comrade Roupen intervened and said, "What did you think? Whoever wants to be in public service should take into consideration that he would be criticized, blamed, and even slapped."

Yeghisapet retorted, "Is that possible? To be slapped, serving them for so long?"

Then Roupen told us the following incident that happened in the Moush District (part of Western Armenia's highlands):

During one of the general fedayeen meetings, and in the presence of Kevork Chavoush,[7] it was decided that the fighters would go underground for a while. It was also decided that intellectual comrades would be sent, each in turn, to the villages to preach the mission of the national liberation movement and convince the villagers to take up arms.

So, I was appointed to go to the "K" village, meet up and talk with the inhabitants, and encourage them to buy guns. I think it was a remote village in the region of Khnous,[8] where the liberation teachings had not reached yet. In everyday, non-fedayi clothes and with a small handgun hidden away, I went to the designated village and introduced myself to the village leader and asked him to gather the young people, so I could talk to them about the national liberation fighters. They gathered in the courtyard of the small church where, whenever possible, using their dialect mixed with Eastern Armenian, I began preaching to them saying, "Your village needs to buy guns," and I even suggested the number of guns needed. "If you are unable to purchase guns," I added, "you can entrust the money to the local leader of the freedom fighters, and he will provide you the necessary guns."

7 Kevork Ghazarian (1870 –1907), commonly known as Kevork Chavush, was an Armenian legendary fedayi in the Ottoman Empire. His main goal was to ameliorate the plight of the Armenian peasantry in the face of harassment by marauding Turks and Kurds. To this end, he advocated armed resistance. Kevork Chavush's extraordinary daring and valor inspired his men as he led the resistance in the region of Daron-Sassoon from 1904 until 1907, when he was killed in battle. (Dasnabedian, 195.)

8 Khenus was a historic Armenian town in the province of Erzurum in the Ottoman Empire. It played an important role during the Armenian national liberation struggle and served as a post on the arms transfer roads.

After listening to me carefully, the village leader who was a giant of a man, came to me and said, "It's good that you are babbling like a teacher, but you can't do anything about liberation dressed in this apparel. Then he slapped me hard and told me to get lost. Fire was spewing from my eyes. What could I have done? I only had a small gun, which I neither would have wanted nor would have used against my compatriots. So dispirited, I returned. Kevork Chavoush, seeing my sad appearance from afar, knew at once that something must have happened. He and Magar of Sbaghan[9] began mocking me, saying, "It looks like this baron (mister) was beaten up by the villagers."

When I told them about the incident, the boys, especially Magar and Avrana Aram, enraged said, "How they could beat up our baron? (They wanted to say 'our leader'.) We must return and teach the village a lesson by punishing them." A wave of agreement spread amongst the freedom fighters.

I answered, "Yes, we need to go and show them our true fedayi selves but not to punish them; instead, we need to win them over and have them serve our cause." Kevork Chavoush and I ordered we all go back to the village in full fedayeen attire and on horseback. They put me in charge to take care of the immediate arrangements.

As we neared the village, we shot in the air in different directions. Thinking that it was a Kurdish attack, the villagers panicked and began to disperse. One of the boys from the hilltop shouted not to flee, that we were only fedayeen. From then on, they greeted us with pleasure and in crowds that one couldn't have imagined. The old men touched and kissed the stirrups of our horses. We gave orders that the men of the village gather in the churchyard. When they came, I again preached that they needed to be armed.

Meanwhile, I had pulled down my fur hat so low that the leader of the village wasn't able to recognize me. When I took it off, the village leader at once came and kneeled in front of me saying, "Sir, let me kiss your feet; forgive me. Hey, man of God, if you had something to say, why

9 Magar was a famous freedom fighter. Born in the village of Sbaghank in Sassoon, he was a close companion to Kevork Chavush and fought alongside him in many battles. Sbaghanats Magar's self-sacrifice and martyrdom was witnessed at the Battle of Petar in Sassoon, where he pleaded to his comrades to leave so that he could secure their backs with the last bullet in his rifle.

didn't you come like a fedayi fighter? Instead, you came like a humble schoolteacher."

I said, "What are you apologizing for, man? Stand up. You did well to have slapped me. You brought me to my senses … I realized that our people, like the Kurds, are impressed by visible and palpable power and wouldn't tolerate a poor teacher's verbal prodding."

As soon as I had finished talking, that giant of the village leader started to yell orders to the villagers saying, "Mgo, give 10 gold coins; you Khacho, you are capable of giving seven." He told another to give 15 gold coins. He ordered some to pay in place of the poor villagers. As for him, he pulled off the kamar (a belt, sometimes with special pockets) and took out more than 100 red gold coins. "This is my share," he said.

I said, "No, we don't need this much." We accepted only the sum we had pre-calculated as fair and just for that village within their financial capabilities. However, that wasn't my only intention. My hope was to have that giant and unique village leader and his young men join the cause of our national liberation. After the villagers dispersed, we shared a meal with the village leader.

Pulling him aside, I said, "You know? I will make you a committee head, and I want you to choose someone from this village who knows how to read and write, and another one who can be dependable and hold on to the committee's funds."

He selected two other people to sit at the meeting with us. After prolonged explanation of our national liberation movement, I took out a red stamp and handed it to them. They kissed it and, calling it sacred, esteemed it worshipfully.

"So, my dear child," continued Roupen, "because of that one slap to my face, that whole village, with its leader and its young men, became one of the centers through which the guns for self-defense were transported. At the end, the government began to suspect and pursue the village leader who joined the fedayeen and, after a heroic life, he too became a victim of the last retreat from Sassoun."

***

On one occasion, Roupen, Yeghisapet, and I were talking about love and married couples in villages and cities. Inevitably, a debate developed. I was arguing that love was different between village couples and city couples. Village couples betrayed one another less than urban couples.

Roupen insisted that love is the same in town or country and that passion did not recognize either city or village dwellers. When the debate got intense, Roupen finally said, "Did you realize that freedom fighters have their own experiences of infidelity?"

Bewildered, we asked him, "How could that be?"

He answered, "I cannot say it in Yeghisapet's presence because the answer is graphic. I can't describe it even in my memoirs, even though it is a very entertaining thing." Referring to his last comments, he started chortling, "Ha-ha-ha." Upon our insistence in relation to the theme under discussion, he recounted the following eye-witness account from the period of national liberation struggle in Western Armenia (1894-1908):

One day we decided to pay a visit to village X, where there was an organized committee. But a military guardhouse was at the entrance of the village, which was a problem because the population was equally divided between Kurds and Armenians. Therefore, it was not possible for us be there during daytime. One of our unequalled khumpabed (group leaders), Avrana Aram (Aram Der Vartanian), was appointed that day's leader. In invasions like this, the group leader would also be the commander, and everyone was obliged to follow his instructions. In case of any mistakes, only the leader could be held responsible.

It was a cold night. Even the small stream that was almost 50 steps away from the guardhouse was frozen. When we were silently crossing the stream, one of our comrades stepped on cracked ice and fell into the stream. His comrades next to him were hardly able to rescue him without making any noise. After crossing the stream and mostly crawling in the dark, we passed the guardhouse and entered the first structure we saw, a barn stored with hay. We unlocked the wooden bolt and went in. We felt that it was only a haybarn, but we didn't know if it belonged to an Armenian or a Kurd.

Avrana Aram said, "Comrades, since we are all soaked, and it is one o'clock in the morning, I suggest we rest and dig inside the straw mound for warmth. But keep your nostrils out to breathe. It is not allowed to cough or sneeze." Aram declared that in the morning for sure someone will come by this barnyard to pick up some fodder to feed the livestock.

If he is Armenian, we will force him to lead us to the committee supervisor's home. If he is a Kurd, we may have to strangle him. Aram stressed that no one moves, whatever happens, until he comes out of the straw.

As ordered, all 15 of us undressed and dug ourselves inside the heaps of straw, next to each other. As our clothes were drying out on the other side of the heap, we were gradually getting warm deep inside the heap itself. After staying like this for a few hours, the door latch creaked open at dawn the next morning, and a girl came inside carrying an oil lamp and a basket. Inside the heap, we held hands, but it wasn't proper to reveal our naked bodies in front of a woman. So we kept quiet.

Having held the light in her hand, she wasn't going to be able to notice us. We were watching her and impatiently waiting for her to take the straw and leave. Filling the basket with straw, she placed the lamp on the ground and sat on the basket filled with straw. She sat there for 5-10 minutes. Nearly 10 minutes later, the door latch again creaked open and in came a young man, making sweet talk to her in Armenian during their lovemaking. After their passion play ended in front of our eyes, first the girl and then the boy with their baskets left the barn.

Barely had they left and unable to wait for Aram's orders, the boys came out laughing. The scene was so funny that no one could have repressed his laughter. Immediately we put on our clothes and again hid in the pile of straw. Half an hour later, someone again came in with a basket, and guess who he was? He was the man we were looking for, the supervisor of the committee.

As soon as Aram and we planted ourselves in front of him, thinking that we were robbers, he was baffled and just stood there. It seemed he was speechless. However, when we were in the light, he at once recognized me and said, "Oh, it's you, Roupen."

After exchanging kisses, he led us to his home next door, an adjacent building, and advised that before sunrise we follow one another in a single row and climb to the floor above. When we were all there, the landlord ordered breakfast to be prepared for us, and the boys were still unable to suppress their laughter.

Half an hour later, when breakfast arrived, guess who was serving it to us? That same girl, who was none other than the wife of our committee supervisor. You should have seen the boys' laughter and amusement.

And our landlord and his wife felt so happy that the boys were so glad to be in their house. They never knew the real reason for our cheeriness.

After spending that day there, we completed our mission. At midnight, with enough food, we headed quietly toward the mountains in a joyous mood.

Comrade Roupen concluded his eyewitness account:

"So you see, Kevo-jan,[10] that love and passion do not differentiate between village or city life. All are the same. Maybe, the city dweller's passion is expressed in a nice room, and the villager in a ... straw barn."

***

On another occasion, he told us the following story:

The Kurdish tribes of Bingueol, whose leader was called Zeynal, were our friends from Kevork Chavoush's time.

It was time for me to reciprocate Zeynal's visit. Because the Kurds are easily impressed by appearance of power, we had to put on a respectable show for our visit. With almost 25 horsemen, together with Vartan Vartabed (the abbot of the St. Garabed Convent[11]) we rode to the mountains of Bingueol[12] to see Zeynal, the tribal leader. When they noticed us from a distance, they came to meet us with a couple of horsemen.

When I came near their house door, a very charming lad, as a sign of respect and holding firmly my horse's reins, put his hand under my foot, so I could dismount. Once inside the house, the same young man removed my boots to wash my feet with the water he had just brought in. As is accepted in the Kurdish customs, we exchanged kind words of welcome, good wishes, and then were invited to sit at the table.

Abbot Vartan translated our conversation between me and the leader. During supper, Zeynal was so enthused that he wanted to make our brotherly friendship permanent. So he suggested we seal our relationship according to their custom. We cut a slit in our palms and clasped

10 Short for Kevork (George). When "jan" is tagged at the end of a name, it means "dear."

11 The St. Garabet Monastery of Mush was founded in the fourth century CE. Archimandrite Vartan was the last abbot of the monastery and the last leader of Daron province who collaborated with all the partisans (Fedayees). He was an influential figure in Sassoon and Daron. He became a martyr in 1915.

12 Bingöl, a town north of the Mush Plain, once had numerous Armenian villages. It is surrounded by mountains and numerous glacier lakes, hence the Turkish name, meaning "a thousand lakes".

hands; our bloods mixed with each other's blood.

The tribesman's wife had passed away. He suddenly said, "Hey, are you married?"

I said I wasn't.

He asked if I had a sister.

"In our country I used to have one, but I haven't heard from her for five years."

"If that's the case," he said, "I promise to give you my daughter as your wife. And you promise, if we stay alive, you will give me your sister as my wife."

I was confused all at once. Beside me, Abbot Vartan urged me in Armenian "Oh, Roupen. Just say yes. Because if you don't, it will be disrespectful."

So I lightheartedly said, "Why not?"

He immediately called the charming young lad, who was his daughter, in reality in boy's clothes. She blushed and kissed my hand.

At the end of our visit and when we were going to leave, the tribesman's daughter, blushing and very charmingly, once again put her hand under my feet so I could mount my horse. Naturally, on our way back, I became the laughingstock among my comrades. Joking, we arrived at our destination, totally forgetting the incident.

Sometime later, when the sultan was forced out by the Young Turk revolutionaries and Constitution was proclaimed and restored in 1908, I was living in Kars with my mother and sister. I was informed that Zeynal wished to see me. Immediately, I recalled the pleasant event and retold/described it to my sister, Mariam, and asked her how to get out of our commitment.

My sister was a sophisticated and educated girl, played the piano magnificently, and could sing well, too. And our house, a mansion, was beautifully decorated. In the middle of the hall was a fountain. And from the ceilings hung crystal chandeliers that reminded you of a church atmosphere. Mariam said "Don't be concerned. I will plan something that the Kurd himself resign himself from his commitment to me.

After the usual greetings and evoking God's name, we started talking about the past and present, using Kurdish, Armenian and Turkish. In fact, he had come so that we would mediate a pardon for him from the newly installed Turkish government (that included ARF members of parliament), as he was still considered a fugitive.

Mariam had prepared such a festive supper and had decorated the living room and the dining room so marvelously ... with plenty of lights that, when the man entered the hall, was stupefied and was looking around him. He began to take off his shoes. Perhaps he thought he was in a mosque or afraid that the beautiful carpets would get soiled.

My sister was wearing the latest fashion. She had makeup on. Her sleeveless dress showed cleavage, and her bare arms were as white as snow. She began saying, "No, my bey, don't take off your shoes. This is your house. Come this way."

In this scenario, Zeynal would not dare lift his head to make eye contact with my sister.

Interrupting Zeyal's confusion, I said, "Zeynal, here, this is my sister Mariam and your fiancée."

The man started shaking his head left and right.

Coming very close to Zeynal, my sister placed soft cushions on his back and said, "Rest. Lean this way for more comfort ...." Before supper, my sister sat at the piano and started playing and singing in her sweet soprano voice.

The Kurd, who hadn't seen such a house nor a festive dinner table, remained astounded, but he remained polite and dignified, appropriate to the status of a tribal leader.

At supper I noticed that the man was hardly eating, and I was sure that he stayed hungry. After supper after my sister had made all the necessary arrangements in the living room, around 10 p.m., the tribesman and I slept in different and beautiful beds and soft mattresses. However, I noticed that the man was unable to sleep. Around midnight I got up, turned on the lights, and saw that the Kurd was awake.

I told him that I was hungry and couldn't sleep and would bring in something to eat. This time I brought different snacks and sat on the carpet. We started eating with our fingers, according to the fedayeen custom. He was eating with such gusto since he had not eaten anything during supper.

Once seated I said, "You know, I am still not used to these soft mattresses. Let's sleep on the floor," to which he eagerly agreed.

When we hit the floor, grabbing our individual blankets from the mattress, this poor man asked, "Does this house really belong to your family?"

I said that it did.

"If you haven't lost your mind, how is it possible you abandon this luxurious comfortable life for years, roaming mountain terrain as a freedom fighter, often sleeping on the ground full of lice and filth?"

I answered that our revolutionary and ideological lives were different and, if need be, I would again abandon this comfortable life and return to my rugged mountain life.

Silent for a second, he said, "Brother, you know I need to tell you something. I know you have the right to be furious and to even kill me. Do you remember our promises we made to one another? I don't consider myself worthy of your sister. This out-of-my-world woman, who is used to this luxurious way of life, would be unable to adjust to our mountainous Kurdish habits and lifestyle. So I beg of you to free me from the obligation of my vow. And, you are free to marry my daughter since you are used to mountain living. Knowing well that breaking my promise is a dishonor to you, take this revolver and punish me as you wish."

Of course, I was ready for this and said, "No need. According to our own tradition, man or woman, boy or girl, are always free to cancel the engagement."

In this way, the question was closed. Zeynal was our guest for several more days. He then returned to the mountains and got married a second time. I haven't heard anything of him since.

Years later during the period of the first Republic of Armenia (1918-1920), when I was the Minister of War, a few patriarchal sheikhs of that tribe had crossed the border to come to see me. With them was the son of the tribal leader Zeynal. They told me that during a battle against one of his enemies, he was about to be captured. The tribal leader, realizing that he would be caught by the enemy, he first killed his wife and daughter and handed his seven- or eight-year-old son to his junior tribal leaders, and ordered them to bring his son to me, and then he killed himself. I tried very hard to keep and educate the boy, but he was like a true cub of a Kurdish lion and refused to stay with me. He ordered his sheikhs to take him back to the mountains. The junior tribal leaders could not disobey the young cub's wishes, and so they departed with this little boy. Since then, I haven't heard from them.

***

This is what my uncle Kevork told me who lived in Jerusalem from 1941 till 1945:[13]

During the Second World War, Roupen Pasha (Der Minassian) Fedayis former leader, the defense minister of the Republic of Armenia (and his wife) lived with us. We used to keep their presence in town a secret from the general public in order to keep them safe from unforeseen and unexpected dangers.
Roupen remained in one of the backrooms. Through my efforts, he was focused on knowing all developing diplomatic and military activities of the war, demanding every detail from me. Because of the nature of my work, I was acquainted with British officers, and every detail of information I snatched from them, I would pass them on to Roupen.
One evening, we were sitting facing one another. I was conveying the news of the day to him when someone knocked on the door. When I opened it, I saw my British colonel friend sprang in front of me with his fellow officers.
It was the time of the Stalingrad[14] (today's Volgograd) German occupation. My colonel-friend said they had come to receive Roupen Pasha's views on the Russo-German War front.
I was surprised that Roupen's hiding place was known to them. Then I went into denial, saying that I don't know anyone by that name and that name means nothing to me. But they insisted so adamantly that I realized it would be futile to persist in my denial.
I doubted if Roupen would ever accept to see those British he abhorred so much. How was I supposed to tell him about their visit? After all, his

13 Kevork recounted WWII Stalingrad battle event to Garo Vahan Manjikian, a nephew who transcribed and published them in 1978. The title: "On Roupen Pasha" (a recollection as spoken by Kevork Manjikian) in Dziler (Buds), the student periodical of Karen Yeppe National College in Aleppo, Syria. This document was not available on 2008 when Armenian edition was published.

14 This battle, a turning point of the war in Europe against Nazi Germany, convinced Hitler that Germany would not be able to destroy Communist Party Rule in Russia; his primary goal for attacking Russia was to destroy Communist Rule.

presence in Jerusalem was supposed to be a well-kept secret.

In desperation, I informed him about the visitors. After listening to his expected litany, a series of biting and sarcastic words, he finally said, “Go ask those British people what they want from a humble son of a small nation.”

Finally, after a prolonged bout of negotiations, Roupen agreed to receive the visitors on one condition: that they hear his views without any comments on them.

Half an hour later, a heated debate had already begun between the two sides. I acted as the translator.

The debate revolved around the battle for the conquest of Stalingrad. Replying to the tone of the questions put by the British, Roupen declared that the German army will witness their greatest defeat at Stalingrad if they stubbornly persist to proceed with an occupation of Stalingrad. While he was speaking, his eyes were focused on the map that the British officers had brought with them.

From their skeptical facial expressions, the British clearly had no respect for Roupen’s opinion. One of the officers even said sarcastically, “What do you understand about modern warfare, since you are only a freedom fighter?”

Roupen was about to tear the Englishman apart. We were barely able to restrain him. A little later, the British officers apologized for the trouble they had caused and left.

Seated: Anna and Roupen (Comrade Roupen Pasha) Der Minassian
Standing left to right: Yeghisapet, Kevork, and Siranoush Der Vartanian.

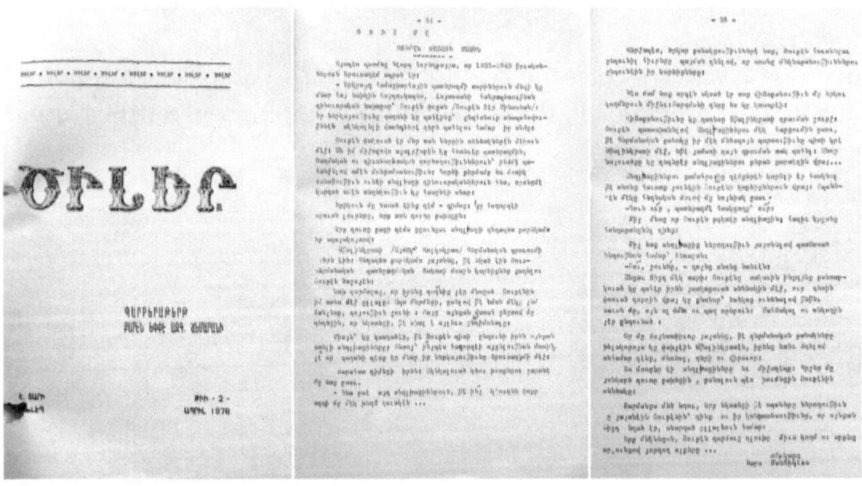

ԾԻԼԵՐ

Garo Manjikian's article in "*Dziler*" (Buds)

"Pooh, dogs!" he shouted behind them.

Exactly one year went by. Roupen kept himself confined to the room we provided. He would sleep on the rug on the floor, covering himself with a thin linen cloth even on cold and wintery days. He would not accept a mattress or a bed.

One day the radio broadcast reported that panicked German troops were fleeing from Stalingrad, leaving behind countless dead and injured and prisoners, abandoning their weapons.

I had forgotten about the visit of the British and the incident. One evening, there was a knock at the door. When I opened it, the same British officers rushed into Roupen's room. I was taken aback with surprise when I realized that the officers were apologizing to Roupen, congratulating him for being so precisely accurate in predicting the decisive outcome of the battle.

When they left, Roupen turned his face away from me and wiped the tears flowing down his cheeks.

***

With this episode of my recollections, I end my memoirs about the days I had spent with Comrade Roupen. They have been so precious and fatherly to me and will remain so. It was a pleasure to sit and listen to Roupen all night long, 'til dawn.

In early 1945, Comrade Roupen left for Beirut to join his sons, who were studying in Beirut. In September 1945, as the Director of Traders and Shippers Company, they sent me to Beirut. I was not able to find a house immediately. Upon Comrade Roupen's insistence, I lived in his house for six months, where we continued our precious conversations. It was in Beirut that Roupen reunited with his beloved revolutionary group leaders, Moushegh and Vartan Shahbaz, who would visit him regularly.

One day Roupen said, referring to Moushegh, "Do you see this humble giant of a man? This man was one of those who cleansed the Republic of Armenia of Turks." Roupen would always tell me, "I will write all my memoirs, but I don't think I could describe the retreat from Sassoun toward Armenia ... that can best be described by Moushegh." The Sassoun Retreat was, in fact, left out of Roupen's memoirs, which was written by Moushegh himself.[15] In spite of Roupen being in command

15 Minassian, pp. 53-122. Pages 82-96 of this volume describe the retreat from Sassoon to Manazkert and

for cleansing Turkish villages, he pretended that he was invisible, rather that his group leaders were the ones who carried out the actions.

One day I made Moushegh talk a bit (he was a man of few words), and he said, "If we had had one other Roupen during the period of the first Republic of Armenia, it would have been certain that not one Turk could even be found in Armenia. That's how great Roupen is. If Aram Manoukian was the one who declared the independence of the republic," Moushegh continued, "Roupen was the one who made it Armenian. We never got a direct order from Roupen to cleanse the villages, but when he had a burdensome job to do for this sensitive and difficult operation, he would call his group leaders and on his famous map would draw circles.[1] Silently, we would understand his intention and would cleanse the denoted regions in the shortest time possible. We would fill them with Armenian immigrants immediately.

Left to right: Levon Pasha Shahoian (ARF, Iraq), Anna and Roupen with Zabel's children Dikran and Vahe, and Ardashes (Zenop's son), Jerusalem, 1943

Yerevan.

1 Der Minassian, pp. 109-110.

"When the inspectors came, we as group leaders would pretend ourselves to be villagers, thus proving to them that this area was not Turkish and moreover that the cemetery was all Armenian. It happened that the regular Armenian army wouldn't let us transport guns. We would tell them that we would obey orders from Roupen directly. While waiting for the order, written on a piece of cigarette paper from Roupen, we would have made the armaments disappear."

In Beirut, I remained the director of my company until November 30, 1946. When my one-year contract ended with that company, I returned to Palestine, this time to Haifa city. As a naval shipping trade specialist, I became the vice president of the Steel Brothers & Co. Ltd., a British company.

Chapter 16
EMIGRANT ONCE AGAIN

Because of the sad events of 1948 between Arabs and Jewish communities of Palestine, 90 percent of the Armenians, along with the local Arabs in Palestine, escaped to neighboring Arab countries (Lebanon, Syria, Jordan). My family and I stayed in Israel because of my job in Haifa.

Massacred Palestinian workers returning from Jerusalem to their village deir yassin, 9 April 1948

During the first period of anarchy, from May to June 1948, the Jewish survivors of the European war began to resettle in Israel and occupy abandoned houses. They would often invade houses where people were still living. In Haifa, no Armenian community national authorities were left (that the St. James Monastery would have appointed).[1] Even the abbot of the Haifa community, appointed by the St. James patriarchate

1 In the churches of the Armenian diaspora, priests in any given city would be appointed by the higher church authority (Patriarch in Palestine — later Israel — or the prelates in other countries). Besides church duties, religious leaders in small Armenian communities would often present the Armenian local community interests to the government authorities. In Shavarsh Kouymian's absence, Kevork and others developed lay community leadership.

of Jerusalem, Archimandrite Shavarsh Kouymjian, fled the country, leaving his parish behind him. His parishioners, who now had no *vartabed* (religious leader), were without leadership to intervene on their community's behalf and, as a result, were subjected to material losses by the incoming Jewish refugees.

Even though I was a newcomer to Haifa, I found a way to gather some 25-30 individuals from the remaining Armenians and convinced them to elect a community institution and to have it legally recognized by the newly formed Israeli State authorities. This initiative was the first of its kind in Palestine, but in that same meeting we planned and prepared an action plan and constitution. A five-member committee was formed by election for a period of three years as a community executive body. We presented this plan to the government immediately, and it was approved.

The members of the First National Executive Body were: chairman, Kapriel Zakarian; secretary, Kevork (George) Manjikian; treasurer, Shnorhq Dadian; advisers, Karekin Yalenezian and Sarkis Ebberian. This executive body actually played a crucial role in the community because every issue or demand was articulated through this institution, which was recognized as legitimate by others. Thanks to this executive body, many of the abandoned properties left behind by those who had fled along with those who remained were saved from state confiscation or theft. Only a year later were we able to get permission from St. James Monastery to bring Vartabed Harutiun Moushian from the St. James Monastery, as the new Armenian priest of Haifa. Later the Patriarch of Jerusalem, Gyuregh, now deceased, appointed Vartabed Moushegh. The Patriarch expressed satisfaction for our activities and encouraged us to continue our work.

When our three-year term was coming to its end, we planned to have elections again for the next three years executive body. But the vicar of the Patriarchate, Bishop Yeghisheh Derderian (Patriarch Gyuregh was deceased by then) absolutely refused to form an executive body through elections. He insisted that at the monastery, according to its traditional customs, he is the one who appoints a national body. He threatened us, saying that if we did not accept his demand then he could recall the Vartabed Moushian and have the church and school shut down.

Ignoring his threat, we went ahead with the elections. Eighty percent of those who were eligible to vote participated in the voting, and 75 percent of those voted on our behalf. So, for the next three years, the following were elected: chairman, George Manjikian; secretary, Shnorhq Dadian; treasurer, Bedros Beboian; and two advisors. This system of civilian election rather than patriarchal appointees continues in Haifa today (1958).

Kevork's residential 3-story building permit, Palestine, 1946; denied by Israeli authorities, 1952

During the time I was in Israel, naturally as a result of emigration, the Armenian community's social, cultural, and political life disappeared. Only a handful of able ARF members were left in Haifa. Some of my associates and I had the burdensome task of reorganizing everything. The HMEM sporting club (the Armenian Sporting General Union) was reorganized after many hours of hard work. My wife Yeghisapet's tenacious efforts helped to re-establish our local Armenian Red Cross branch. These two sister organizations had their distinct clubs where, as before, and with joint forces all national celebrations would take place. By organizing excursions and meetings, we were able to revitalize Armenian life within the community.

Only four ARF party comrades remained in Haifa. This number gradually increased each year. By the time I left Haifa, Israel, in 1954, our group had 18 members. The Israeli government would not allow us to have any direct relations with sister organizations in Arab countries, so I sent our reports to the Cyprus National ARF Committee. The report of our activities during those times (1948-1954) could be found in the archives of the Cyprus ARF Committee. Moreover, the number of HMEM members increased from 12 to 60. The membership of ladies in the Red Cross also rose from 14 to 42.

All these were achieved thanks to several selfless community members. Because of the lack of capable people, I was facing a very difficult task. For example, I was a rotating Party chairman and, at the same time, I was the HMEM President of Honor (an advisor) and the ARF committee representative of the Red Cross branch. My presence was mandatory on the panel of the speakers during each celebration, banquet, or gathering. I felt a sense of contentment carrying out my responsibilities and carried them out with pleasure until August 1954, when I was forced to leave Israel for Beirut, hoping to settle there for good.

In the Ashrafieh district in Beirut, I joined the ARF Balakian Committee as a regular member. Because of my work, I am in no position to accept any executive responsibility. Currently, I am employed by Boustros & Co., a trading company, responsible for their correspondence and accounting.

Kevork Manjikian
1958, Beirut

EPILOGUE

My uncle, Kevork Manjikian, remained in the newly created state of Israel and continued his work within the same company in Haifa. He and his wife Yeghisapet worked very hard to restore the local Armenian community life that had deteriorated due to the recent upheavals and emigration of a great number of Armenians from the city. He had to constantly deal with newly established government authorities, both for community and personal affairs.

Hagop Hovsep Manjikian, his junior uncle Nishan, on the bow of Kevork's fishing boat, Beirut 1955

A vexing problem was his possession of a parcel of land on which illegal construction started in 1952 by Jewish immigrants. He became embroiled with legal and municipal authorities to defend his rights with no results. Essentially his property was stolen from him. He was utterly disappointed from the state authorities and started seriously thinking to leave Israel. He was able to negotiate his leave with special permission to take all his belongings with him to Beirut — permission rarely granted at the time to emigrants going out from Israel.

After a lifetime spent in Palestine and then in Israel, my uncle and his wife moved to Beirut in 1954, with the intention of settling there "for good." His brother, Nishan, and his sister, Zabel, with their families were also living in Beirut after they fled Palestine during the Arab-Israeli War of 1948. Nishan had to hire trucks and meet Kevork and wife at the border between Israel and Lebanon to transfer their belongings from Israeli to Lebanese trucks.

Kevork and Yeghisapet with relatives, Port of Beirut, 1955

It was a great joy for all of us to greet Kevork and Yeghisapet after many years of separation, and it was a big relief for them to be close to loved ones.

In Beirut, Uncle Kevork was busy with different kinds of work (accounting, bookkeeping, correspondence), along with involvements in Armenian community life. The most remarkable in its scope was his fishing ship enterprise. With a Palestinian friend Kevork had met while working for the shipping company Prince Line, they bought and modified a sailboat into a huge wholesale fishing vessel with modern equipment and a new and powerful motor. The fishing nets had a diameter of tens of meters and could reach the depths of the sea to gather a great number of fish, which were then raised onto the ship with motorized equipment.

The ship had a captain, sailors, and workers. Fishing took place in the open seas. The ship sailed as far as the seaside of Port Said — or wherever they heard there would be plentiful fish. The ship would return to the harbor loaded with hundreds of boxes of fish, neatly laid in ice and ready to be taken to the merchants in the market.

But in Beirut this unique large-capacity fishing enterprise was frowned upon by the local retail fishermen, who thought that their source of income was in jeopardy because of this modern and plentiful way of supplying fish. As a result, the Lebanese government bodies imposed pressure and threats upon my uncle's business. Finally, he and his partner were obliged to sell the ship, on condition that it must serve a totally different purpose. These developments, of course, had a negative effect financially and emotionally. After that my uncle stayed busy with accounting and correspondence jobs.

Everyday work was a pleasure for him; he had to get out of the house, meet people, and do something useful. That something useful was often helping someone — writing a letter, filling out an application form, accompanying a relative or a friend to a government body or an office to help solve an issue.

For a certain time, Yeghisapet worked as a private nurse in the American University of Beirut Hospital. Under her care were Lebanese government officials and the Late Catholicos Zareh of the Holy See of Cilicia, whom she served both in the hospital and at the Catholicosate in Antelias.

In 1958, when Kevork Manjikian was writing his memoirs, Lebanon was under threat of civil and regional war. Everyone had to stay home, glued to the radio to listen to the sad news. This period was followed by the glorious days in Lebanon, until 1975 when civil war erupted in Lebanon.

Unfortunately, settling in Beirut "for good" was not the final destination for this Manjikian couple. One more move: this time to faraway United States of America, where his brother, Nishan, and his family had long since settled (Nishan had passed away years ago). Both of his sisters, Sara and Zabel, with their families were equally settled in the USA.

As they aged, Kevork and Yeghisapet lived a peaceful life in Los Angeles. Relatives and friends visited them frequently and cared for them. Kevork passed away on March 31 in 1985, and Yeghisapet on July 21, 1991. Sisters Sara and Zabel have since passed away as well.

Three brothers (left to right): Kevork, Hovsep and Nishan Manjikian, Beirut, Lebanon, 1955

And so, that faraway land became the final destination of the orphans who had walked from their villages to Jordan to Jerusalem, and, for Kevork, then to Port Said, back to Aleppo, Kessab then to Beirut, to Palestine, again to Beirut and finally to America. Kevork's mother and older brother are the only ones of the large family buried in their birthplace of Kessab — a concise picture of many such families who were survivors of the Genocide.

The Manjikian couple always kept a cheerful and lively atmosphere inside their home. Although they didn't have any children, throughout the years, someone dear was present as a son or daughter of their household, who enjoyed their care, education, and love. The undersigned was the last in line.

It was another fortunate circumstance for their readiness to become a godfather and a godmother to the weddings of relatives and friends or to the newborns. The family of the undersigned were among those fortunate people. They had godchildren in different cities and always enjoyed their love and respect.

Yeghisapet and Kevork, Beirut

A last glance at Yeghisapet Manjikian, known to all of us as "Auntie." She will always be remembered as a robust and caring person, who always had time and energy to extend a helping hand to people around her and to console them and encourage them. She should be remembered also as a conscious and devoted Armenian woman. She was informed and involved in solving the ups and downs of the national Armenian life, from the confines of the Armenian Red Cross or personally. Her age, precarious health, or her relatives' admonitions did not stop her from participating in the demonstration walk for the commemoration of the 50th anniversary of the Armenian Genocide, from the Genocide Memorial in Bikfaya to the Catholicosate in Antelias, Lebanon.

Hagop Hovsep Manjikian
2022, Montreal, Canada

Kevork manjikian's family (4th and 5th generations), Karadouran, 1928
Seated left to right: Yeghisapet and Zabel
Standing left to right: Kalila (Yaralian) with husband Hovsep, Kevork, Nishan, and Sara

Kevork's Extended Family (4th, 5th and 6th generations), Beirut, Lebanon, 1955

APPENDIX: THE MANJIKIANS, FIVE GENERATIONS

Compiled by Hagop Hovsep Manjikian

I. Oral History

It is thought that the ancestors of the Manjikians have come from Cilicia, most probably from Hadjen, Turkey, but it is unclear what lineage they belonged to and what their family name had been.

This is what Hovhannes Yessayi Manjikian (Toroon Bebo), one of our senior grandfathers, told us how our forefathers had settled in Kessab and established a dynasty there, as transcribed in 1956:

During the Cilician King Levon VI's reign, when the kingdom of Cilicia was weakening, the fortress at Sis remained the only safe haven. The King, with his people's nobility and his army retreated there. The Mamluk Sultan seized this opportunity, entered Cilicia, and besieged Sis. Realizing the Armenian King's resistance, he sent delegates to him and promised him to keep the city standing and to not harm its people, as long as he took the king prisoner. The king believed the Sultan's delegates and, because he loved his people, he gave himself up. But the Sultan didn't keep his promise. Along with Levon VI,[1] he also took 400 members of the nobility, the intelligentsia, and government officials as

1 "...Leo VI, the crowned king in 1374, had to resist the assaults of the Aleppo Emirate. Anticipating that the Pope Gregory XI would not keep his promise of supporting Cilicia, the Mamluks confidently crossed the border of the Armenian kingdom. Leo VI was unable to hold back the Mamluks and sheltered in the citadel of Sis lying on a hard-to-access rock. Even though the Mamluks weren't able to conquer the citadel, they one day managed to severely wound Leo with an arrow. Running out of food and energy, the population of Sis began to consider handing over the citadel. However, Leo soon received a letter from the emir, in which he and his family were guaranteed to be spared if he surrenders the city. Realizing the futility of further resistance, Leo put a stop to it and was taken to Cairo along with his family, Catholicos Poghos I, and the majority of the Cilician princes. This ended Leo's 7-month rule over Cilicia, marking the end of the Armenian Kingdom of Cilicia as well." (Art-A-Tsolum, https://allinnet.info/history/leo-vi-the-last-ruler-of-the-armenian-kingdom-of-cilicia/)

prisoners as well. And so, our forefather, circa 1375, having been in that 400, was taken prisoner. However, it is unclear under what qualification. The Sultan, with his prisoners, arrived at the Syrian city of Hama. Here, some of the prisoners and our forefather got away. It seems that there were a lot of people who escaped. They made their way northwest and settled in the following areas: Ghenemiyeh, Aramoo, Kneh, Yacoubiyeh; but our forefather, with a few others, went to Eski-Yoran (Nerki-Kyugh, one of the first villages in Kessab region). His friends were the Garboushians (Hajaghbints), Panajian, Shekhougian (Shkhgunts) and Itkouanian families' forefathers. (The last family's ancestors has no heirs.) The newcomers to Nerki-Kyugh started to cultivate the land and keep goats. The cultivated land and buildings of present day Kessab used to be a dense forest, where the goats were herded. One day, a shepherd noticed that a goat's goatee was wet. This meant that the goat was near a fountain and had drunk from it. The next day, the shepherd followed the same goat and found the fountain. This was how the fountain source was discovered in Kessab.

It was because of this fountain that the inhabitants of Nerki-Kyugh slowly moved upward and settled in the nearby areas of present day Kessab. Here, people had more suitable and natural conditions and, in case of danger, they would have quickly found shelter in the nearby mountains. They had protection near the forest and had been able to use the water and the angular and strong position of the mountain to their advantage. Here they built houses and founded a village for future permanent settlements. Our forefather's house is thought to have been built behind what is today the library building.

Our forefather was married and had a family in this newly built village. His wife's ancestry is not known. The name of his son, Yessayi, and the members of his family were mentioned. So our great-great grandfather about whose life and family members we have clear information about for the first time, was Yessayi, famously known as "Aysig Bebo," the founder of the Manjikian Dynasty.

Great-great grandfather Yessayi was a clever and ingenious man. He was a merchant, who traveled different places, especially to Egypt. He had signed a trade agreement with the Missirlian family forefather, who had put up a big portion of the capital. From that time onward, tobacco became the major export in the Kessab area. Great-great grandfather Yessayi and his partner bought the tobacco harvests from the villagers, transported them to the seashore of the village of Karadouran, from where they got to Egypt by boats and sailboats.

Apart from being a seaport, Karadouran was our forefather's farm, with its arable and rich fertile soils in the valley. The farm was particularly suitable for the cultivation of tobacco. This region didn't have a populated settlement right away. This fertile valley had remained a distant farm for those villagers who lived in Kessab. But it is told that because of an incident, people set up settlements there:

The Kessab region was a forested and wild area where wild animals lived. One day, in Maghariye (little cave), in what is today the northern entrance to Kessab, a hyena had attacked a villager. After this incident, and after some attempts of trying to find a safer place, Karadouran was recognized as one of the convenient places where they found the remains of an old settlement, too. One of those who had settled down in Karadouran was Great-great grandfather Yessayi, considering his trips that took place from the Karadouran seashore.

The voyage from Kessab to Egypt was frequent and quite profitable for the merchants among our predecessors, Manjikians and Misirilians. In order to be more profitable, Great-great grandfather Yessayi tried to look for ways, so he became friends with the Sultan of Egypt and his royals and one day invited them to a dinner party. Being a clever man with vast experience, he waited at the table and had prepared the food. The Sultan with his princes and entourage, foreign dignitaries from Italy, France, and England were present at the dinner party.

The guests, especially the European officials, were very satisfied with the prepared dishes and wanted to know who cooked and served them. When Great-great grandfather Yessayi presented himself to them, an Italian showed his astonishment by calling out, "Buono mangiare!" The guests left feeling content and from then on, the tobacco trade was conducted much easier by the merchants of Kessab.

Upon return back to Kessab, the forefather of the Misirilians had recounted several times the above-mentioned incident here and there and of course, had mentioned what the Italian had exclaimed. Later in his or his people's Armenian dialect, it changed to "Bon Manjik." As a result, our forefather took up the "Manjik" nickname, and this was how he was known by the villagers. And so, our surname came from that nickname, and the successors of Great-great grandfather Yessayi were called Manjikian.

The Manjik nickname was also given to Great-great grandfather Yessayi's son, Hovhannes. Until now, many know Grandfather Hovhannes as "Manjik Bebo," whose grave is found in the gardens across from the Manjikian Quarterin Karadouran. The latter is erroneously confused with Great-great grandfather Yessayi and the above-mentioned incident is referred to, by mistake, as being Grandfather Hovhannes's story.

Great-great grandfather Yessayi was married to a girl from the Kortian family. From this marriage, Yessayi had seven sons, all of whom became portly and huge men, except for the youngest, who was a delicate and skinny boy. Unfortunately, the six large-framed brothers became infected with a deadly illness, which at that time was known as mouohe or sechanillete (probably malaria). The only one who survived was his youngest son, Hovhannes, despite being the most delicate.

Great grandfather Hovhannes married a girl from the Matossian family and also had seven sons, who were named after his father and his dead brothers. The oldest son was named Yessayi, after his father. The other sons were named in his dead brothers' honor in descending order from the oldest to the youngest brother: Boghos, Garabed, Gergeoss (George, Kevork, also famously nicknamed "Vardem"), Mateos, Panos, Moussa. He also had three daughters, one of whom, whose name is unknown, married to Hagop Yacoubian; the second whose name is also unknown, married to Kevork Titizian, and the third one, Dzakan, possible Dzaghganoush, married to Hovhannes Karaoghlanian.

These seven brothers, in turn, married and set up the foundation for seven new branches of the families, and the Manjikian Dynasty started to expand into seven more branch families. These families were named in their fathers' names, like this, starting with the eldest: the Aysints, the Boughousints, the Gerebidints, the Gergeosints, the Matissints, the Penissints, the Mousamounts (Uncle Mousa's) families. Every family occupied a separate district, which at present are also known as Ayselek, Gergeouslek, Penisslek, etc. The people also use some other forms to name the families: Aysigammounk, Boughousammounk, Gergeossammounk, etc., taking into consideration the ammo (uncle) title.

***

These seven families multiplied and augmented. The Manjikian dynasty progressively became, if not the most, one of the extended dynasties in Kessab. Unfortunately, today, only an insignificant number of the Manjikians live in Karadouran or in the region of Kessab. Between 1946-1947, a noticeable number emigrated to Armenia. The movement to bigger cities and far away countries to study, to start a new career, or to create a new life continues to this day. The Manjikians have spread farther away to large cities in Syria and Lebanon, to countries in the Persian Gulf, Australia, the United States of America, Canada, France.

Many have thought of creating the Manjikian Family Tree, but such a plan has not yet been realized. The day-by-day continuous centrifugal current makes it difficult to make this project come true. In 1956, in my turn, I started gathering some information but my work, too, is unfinished. There are, however, my handwritten stories told to me by Grandfather Hovhannes — Toroon Bebo — and the information he had provided regarding the family tree up to 1956.

The drafted family tree information in tabular form covers close to 30 pages. They contain the recorded handwritten notes with added data collected after 1956. Information from Kessabtsis phonebooks, published in Kessab and Los Angeles, have been used as well as information I gathered on my visit to Karadouran in September 2010.

The approximate dates of births and deaths of the first few generations of the seven ancestral families have been recorded from what Grandfather Hovhannes, Toroon Bebo, had remembered and which need to be verified by comparing them with written records, if they exist. The currently recorded information are preliminary steps for building a Manjikian family tree. It is desirable that this work be continued and persevered. The chart below shows the first Five generations only and Kevork's lineage.

II. Manjikian Genealogy

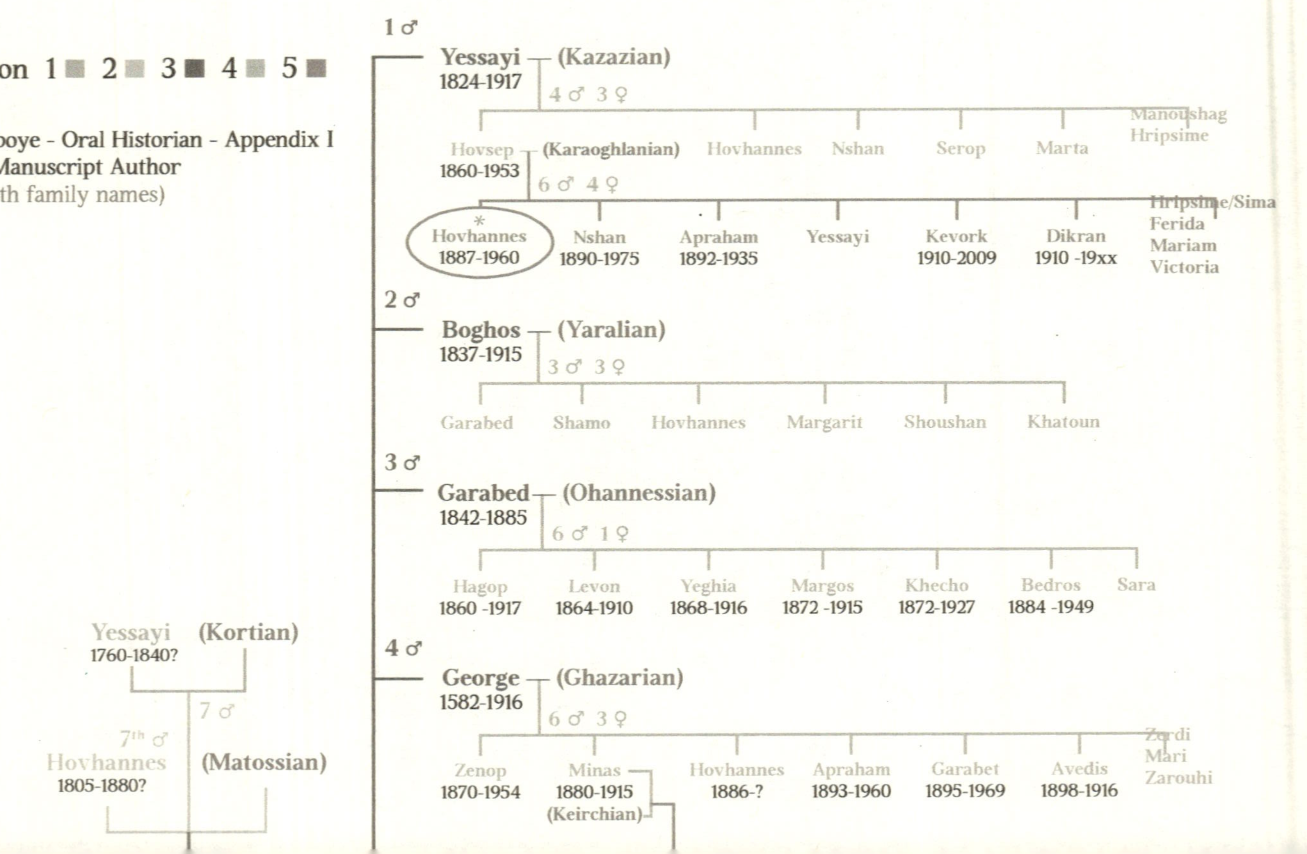

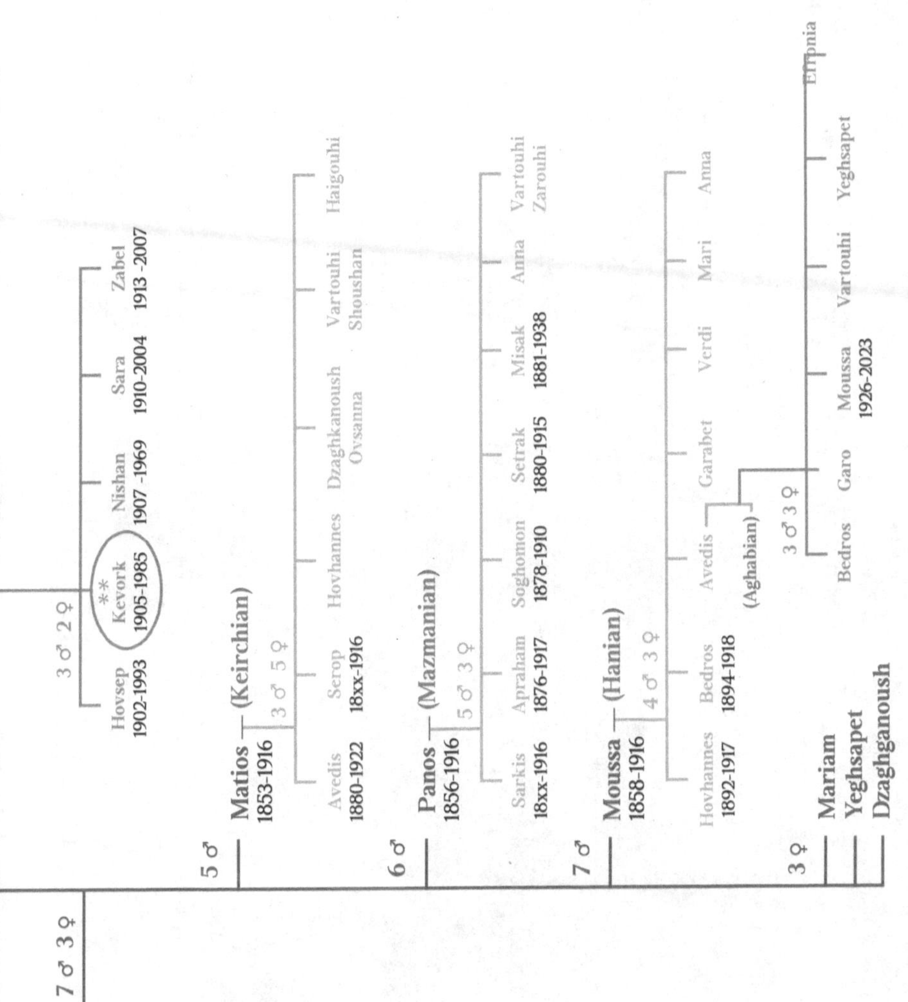
7♂ 3♀
5♂
Matios — (Keirchian)
1853-1916
3♂ 5♀
Avedis
1880-1922
Serop
18xx-1916
Hovhannes
Dzaghkanoush
Ovsanna
Vartouhi
Shoushan
Haigouhi
3♂ 2♀
Hovsep
1902-1993
**
Kevork
1905-1985
Nishan
1907 -1969
Sara
1910-2004
Zabel
1913 -2007
6♂
Panos — (Mazmanian)
1856-1916
5♂ 3♀
Sarkis
18xx-1916
Apraham
1876-1917
Soghomon
1878-1910
Setrak
1880-1915
Misak
1881-1938
Anna
Vartouhi
Zarouhi
7♂
Moussa — (Hanian)
1858-1916
4♂ 3♀
Hovhannes
1892-1917
Bedros
1894-1918
Avedis
(Aghabian)
Garabet
Verdi
Mari
Anna
3♂ 3♀
Bedros
Garo
Moussa
1926-2023
Vartouhi
Yeghsapet
3♀
Mariam
Yeghsapet
Dzaghganoush

Kevork and Yeghisapet Manjikian

www.ingramcontent.com/pod-product-compliance
Lightning Source LLC
LaVergne TN
LVHW090608110826
845146LV00001B/307

* 9 7 9 8 9 8 5 9 8 0 7 0 7 *